THE DEVIL:

DOES HE EXIST?
AND WHAT DOES HE DO?

BY

FATHER DELAPORTE,

OF THE SOCIETY OF MERCY

Translated from the Sixth French Edition.

TAN BOOKS AND PUBLISHERS, INC.
Rockford, Illinois 61105

✠

Recommended:

L. G. De SEGUR,

Bishop of St. Denis.

1871.

Originally published in English in 1871. Reprinted in 1978 by Marian Publications, South Bend, Indiana and in 1980 by Mater Dei Publications, Inc., Arcadia, California.

ISBN: 0-89555-173-X

TAN BOOKS AND PUBLISHERS, INC.
P.O. Box 424
Rockford, Illinois 61105

1982

TRANSLATOR'S PREFACE.

———————

THE valuable and interesting little work now first presented to the public in an English form, appeared, some two or three years since, in France, where it passed through several editions in the space of a few weeks. Its popularity was immense, notwithstanding that other and larger works of a similar nature were already extant. Soon after its appearance, it was brought under my notice by an esteemed missionary priest of this city, a member of the same community as the reverend and learned author. I at once commenced its translation, which was soon unhappily interrupted by severe and protracted family affliction. After many attempts to continue the translation, I have at length succeeded in accomplishing my task, and now present Father Delaporte's admirable little work to the American public. If it only interests readers as much it did myself in translating it, it will be no less popular here than in France.

NEW YORK, Nov., 1871.

LETTER OF Mgr. De SEGUR

TO THE AUTHOR.

REVEREND FATHER:

If every one busied himself with the Devil as you do, the affairs of God would gain by it. You doubtless know the curious saying of Voltaire: "Satan is all Christianity." Hence it was that the unbelievers of the last century sought to destroy, as far they could, belief in the Devil and his works. They succeeded but too well; and it is not unusual to meet now-a-days, even amongst practical Christians, people who scarcely believe in the existence of Satan. Amid all these follies and impiety, Spiritualism again brings forward a little the existence of the Devil and the Angels : and we, the children of the Church, ought to profit by this strange intervention of evil spirits on the earth, to derive from it, at least, this advantage—that henceforth people will believe in the personal existence of Satan and the demons. Your excellent little book will contribute, among others, to bring about this precious result. I join all your friends in felicitating you thereon, and in wishing this work the circulation it deserves.

L. G. DE SEGUR,

Bishop of St. Denis.

CONTENTS.

CONTENTS.

Prayer
Before Reading

COME, Holy Spirit, fill the hearts of Thy faithful and enkindle in them the fire of Thy love.

℣. Send forth Thy spirit and they shall be created.

℟. And Thou shalt renew the face of the earth.

Let Us Pray.

O God, Who didst instruct the hearts of the faithful by the light of the Holy Spirit, grant us by the same Spirit to have a right judgment in all things and ever to rejoice in His consolation. Through Christ our Lord. Amen.

Indulgence of five years. Plenary indulgence, under the usual conditions, if the prayer has been recited daily for a month.

Enchiridion Indulgentiarum, 287.

THE ANGELIC SALUTATION
—

Hail Mary, full of grace, the Lord is with thee; blessed art thou among women, and blessed is the fruit of thy womb, Jesus. Holy Mary, Mother of God, pray for us sinners, now and at the hour of our death. Amen.

THE DEVIL:

DOES HE EXIST? AND WHAT DOES HE DO?

———•———

I.

IMPORTANCE OF THE QUESTION.

DEAR reader, what are you actually doing on earth? You are journeying towards the house of your eternity, the door of which, at some turn of the way, death will throw open. To find in that new and final abode what your heart desires, HAPPINESS, religion, conscience, humanity, all warn you that you must "go about doing good," as did the Man-God, our Master and our Model. The incomparable privilege of free-will was only given you to put you in the way of doing good. Are you convinced of this?

—Assuredly. Is the practice of virtue honorable?—Evidently. Is the practice of virtue conformable to our true interests?—Undoubtedly it is; under a just and good God, to do good is the sure and only means of attaining to true happiness. This all must admit; yet how does it happen that we so often commit evil, which brings us neither happiness nor real profit? *Something* or *some one* invites, solicits, entices us. The way of virtue is not always smooth and pleasant. It presents obstacles against which we may have to struggle. The kingdom of heaven—that is to say, a happy immortality—is the prize of exertion; the brave alone win it. The life of man on earth is a warfare. Either a soldier of virtue, with the hope of a Divine reward, or the slave of vice, under threat of Divine chastisement; there is nothing between.

Dear reader, I ask you not to which side your heart inclines. You reject with horror the slavery of vice; you are a soldier of virtue, a soldier of duty, a soldier of God. What is requisite for the soldier who would fain conquer?—Courage. Yes, but courage alone is not sufficient; prudence is also required. Prudence demands that we apply ourselves to know our enemies, their relative strength, their tactics, the weapons they most dread—in a word, that we acquire that science, which, guiding courage, secures victory. Now, a voice which commands the attention even of those who, unhappily, ignore the infallible voice of God, the voice of Christianity, clearly indicates the several enemies of our souls. "Often," it tells us, "you will find in yourselves, in human society, and even in the material world, incitements to infringe on duty." But the principal sower of evil here below, the tempter most formidable, because the most skillful and the most active, is the reprobate spirit whom popular language, following the Gospel, calls the *Devil;* that is, the *divider*, the *over-*

thrower, the *disperser*, the *destroyer*. This great adversary once put to flight, the combat is mere play; if, on the other hand, he prevails, all is lost. He has made innumerable victims. You, yourself, shall one day increase the sad list, if you neglect the arms which Jesus Christ and His Church have prepared for you. By Jesus Christ you can resist, overcome, escape the gloomy kingdom of Satan, and receive, in heaven, the conqueror's palm. Away from Jesus Christ, you are the sure prey of Satan.

Such is Catholic teaching. It sufficiently indicates that the question of the Devil is not only a curious question, but a practical question of the greatest importance.

II.

IS IT CERTAIN THAT THE DEVIL EXISTS?

To most of our readers this question appears superfluous; but we write for every one, and in an age when people deny the existence of God without being sent to the lunatic asylum. Yes, certainly, there is an Evil Spirit, and even a multitude of evil spirits. For a time, at least in Europe, the devils avoided attracting attention. The philosophy of the eighteenth century had made the grossest materialism fashionable; people became accustomed to believe only what was palpable. Naturally, the Devil agreed to be forgotten, provided God was also forgotten. But materialism is too base, too absurd to last. Faith in God, a moment obscured, shone forth with renewed lustre. No sooner it slept than it awoke; this strange and terrible actor, banished for a time to the region of fancy, reappeared on the scene, and made himself talked of more than ever.

But where are the proofs of his existence?

1. *In the unanimous belief of mankind.*

In the beginning, say, with the Catholic Church, with the Jewish Synagogue, with the heretical and schismatical sects, the traditions of all nations, the Supreme Being created three sorts of beings: material beings, spiritual beings, and man, composed of spirit and of matter. Among the pure spirits, several, having revolted against the Creator, lost, by their crime, the sovereign good. Once condemned, they became obstinate in evil, and incited man thereto. The Bible, which often mentions these evil spirits, names their chief Satan, *Beelzebub*, *Lucifer ;* it calls themselves *bad angels*, *demons* (a word which in the ancient authors sometimes means simply spirits,) and *devils*.

This belief makes manifest a providential plan so harmonious that it would of itself impress calm right reason. Above the created universe, the INFINITE SPIRIT, whose thought conceived and whose power created all things. In the universe, all below, beings that reflect, without knowing them, the perfections of the Creator.

These beings form an ascensional ladder, from step to step of which beauty goes on ever increasing. All above, beings who not only reflect, but know the perfections of the Supreme Being, and live a life like unto His—a life of intelligence, love, freedom. And, forming the tie between these two orders, *humanity*, which, by the body, dips into the material world, and, by the soul, enters into the spiritual world. In a word, matter—spirit soldered to matter—spirit disengaged from matter; there is a complete whole. These three parts of the universe must not be detached one from the other, as there would then be several universes; all are connected together—the material world, the human world, the spiritual world. If spiritual beings remain attached to the Supreme Good, they attract us toward it; if they depart from it, they turn us away from it.

If, then, any one reason falsely, it is not mankind, for mankind believes in good and bad spirits; it is the individual who admires himself so very much that he can no more understand the possibility of a created being whose perfection exceeds his own.

2. The belief of mankind is based on the Divine Word itself. For our sacred books speak often of the Devil, and St. John formally affirms not only that he exists, and that sinners are under his influence, but also that "the Son of God appeared, that He might destroy the works of the Devil." (Eph. I, chap. III.)

As every spirit—not excepting our soul, which is not seen by the corporal eye—makes itself known by acts which can be attributed only to it, so (as we shall soon see) the demons have a thousand times manifested their existence by acts which cannot possibly be ascribed either to man, whom they strike, and whose power they exceed, or to God or the good spirits, to whose sanctity they are opposed.

The existence of evil spirits is, therefore, certain.

The demons are guilty and reprobate spirits.

The Manichæans, ancient heretics, audaciously taught the existence of a *Principle of Evil*, eternal as God, the Principle of Good—of a being thoroughly evil, in perpetual opposition to God. Monstrous error! Good alone is eternal and necessary. Evil is the fall of a being which came forth good from the Creator's hand. When that fall is voluntary, and consequently criminal, it is named sin. God tolerates evil—for a time—in order to offer a glorious field for the exercise of virtue. But it is absurd to imagine that creatures may go on unceasingly insulting the Creator; the hour of justice comes.

Satan is no longer, as modern romancers in religion and philosophy have dreamed, a mere allegorical personification of Sin, as the Muse is of Poetry or History. From Epicurus and Lucretius to Hugo and Littré, Taine and Renan, Atheists have been almost alone in denying the existence of the Devil. Their denial is easily understood. How should the wilfully blind, who no longer see even the sun, whose splendor all proclaim, perceive darkened, extinguished stars? But the Atheists and some few Deists are nothing before the Church, humanity, and the innumerable facts collected and attested by history.

The demons are very real beings, but mere creatures. Originally they made part of the glorious army of the heavens, that is to say, of the angelic hosts, who, in the morning of creation, praised God in gladness, and of whom the army of stars is the magnificent symbol. Like us, but before us, the pure spirits were put to the proof. Stronger and more enlightened than man, the angels who failed in their duty were less excusable than man; hence they were irrevocably deprived of the Divine gifts, and forever separated from the Creator.

A child was asked, "Who created the angels?" The answer was easy: "God." "But who created the Devil?" The child reflected a while, then exclaimed: "God made him an angel; he made himself a devil." Without knowing it, that child spoke as did the Church in the first canon of the fourth council of Lateran.

In what did the crime of the demons consist? That is not precisely known, nor is it necessary that it should be known. According to grave theologians, the future incarnation of the Word was announced to the angels. Lucifer, their chief, refused to humble himself before the future Christ, inferior to him by his human nature, and drew into his rebellion a great number of spirits. Others have thought, with St. Thomas, that Lucifer and his accomplices deemed themselves able, by their own strength, to attain to *supernatural bliss*, and wished to gain it without the aid of their Creator. What is certain is, that they lost this *beatitude* for having, in the trial proposed to their free will, taken the haughty part of disobedience.*

* What is *supernatural bliss*, the end of angels and of men? A very simple comparison will explain this fundamental point of religion : A prince had a number of servants. To all he owes justice ; on all he can bestow gifts. If he abide by that, what happiness soever he may make them enjoy, their condition will not change. But by a spontaneous act of goodness he addresses himself to several amongst them, and says : "It is my will that, henceforth, you shall be no more my servants, but shall be called, and shall really be, my children." This is an admirable change of condition ; as sons of the great king, they are henceforth entitled, if they are faithful to Him, not to receive a salary proportionate to their work, but to share in the paternal wealth and glory. So God, in ordaining men and angels to be His sons, and furnishing them with means superior to the natural capacity of created beings, (by creation mere servants,) displays an infinite charity. He who knows how to correspond therewith shall participate eternally in the blissful life of God himself ; he who despises it, or deserves to be deprived of it, exposes himself to a just and terrible punishment.

III.

DID THE REBELLIOUS SPIRITS, IN FALLING FROM HEAVEN, LOSE ALL?

No. They lost all their felicity; they did not lose all their power. Deprived of their personal gifts, they were not deprived of the faculties inherent in their nature.

Even in the bravest armies, it sometimes happens, that a soldier fails in his duty and commits a crime. Then he is degraded, stripped of the uniform and the decorations he has dishonored; he is put in irons; he is declared for ever unworthy to march under the banner; he has no more right to the noble title of soldier; all the personal advantages which he enjoyed are taken away from him. He retains, nevertheless, his nature as man; he has, as before, eyes to see, hands to act, understanding to know, and a will to determine. So the demons, after their

revolt had caused them to be expelled
from heaven, remain such as they were
originally constituted, that is to say,
beings with an intelligence and a power
superior to the intelligence and power
of man.

God made created beings to live one
with the other. The universe is the hus-
bandman's field, wherein the good grain
and the tares grow together till the har-
vest time. In a family, virtuous children
increase the general welfare, vicious children diminish it; all dwell under the
same roof. Only, the wise and prudent
father closely watches the latter, and
restrains, when necessary, their evil designs. So it is with Providence. Each
one of the angels received, at the beginning, his share of power. That of the
rebels has not been destroyed; they remain actors in the universal drama, as
the wicked, their imitators, in the social
drama. Instead of being face to face
with us, the ministers of light and peace,

they are the ministers of trial and punishment. A devil overwhelmed Job with tribulations; he proved him, and embellished his crown. Another devil destroyed the first husbands of Sara, because that they, in a holy union, had sought only the gratification of their passions; he executed the decrees of Divine Justice. The malice of the demons, in despite of itself, glorifies God by contributing to the execution of His adorable will.

IV.

IF THE EVIL SPIRITS ARE IN HELL, HOW CAN THEY TROUBLE THE EARTH?

There is a Hell, a "place of torments." (St. Luke, xvi, 28.) "Christians rightly think," says the Pagan philosopher Celsus, "that those who live holily shall be rewarded after death, and that the wicked shall undergo eternal torments. This belief is, furthermore, common to them and all others." Since the time of Celsus, great efforts have been made to get rid of the belief in hell, but without success. Truth remains. A light-brained skeptic wrote one fine morning to Voltaire : " I have succeeded in proving that there is no Hell." " You are very fortunate," replied Voltaire ; "I am far from that." It is fashionable now-a-days to ignore hell, and the spirit-rappers and writers of our day unanimously favor this delusion, very acceptable to all those who do not like pain either in this life or the other ; but the justice of God, like human justice, has its prison. This prison is called Hell.

To it the devils ought to be banished. But the Divine Word, and the Church, who is its interpreter, say not that all the wicked spirits are, since their fall, in Hell, but only that " everlasting fire" was "prepared for the Devil and his angels." Being spirits, the devils do not need to be chained in one place to undergo their punishment; they bear it wheresoever the Creator permits them to be and to act. The good angels who assist us see the face of God, and bear with them everywhere the celestial beatitude. In like manner, the demons everywhere undergo their damnation, and several of them, if not all, act on earth. Proofs of this are on every page of Sacred and Profane History.

Let us first consult the Holy Scriptures:

Satan speaks to Eve in the terrestrial paradise; Satan goes about through the world, and witnesses the sublime virtue of Job, whom he obtains permission to subject to the most severe trials; many devils enter into the bodies of the possessed whom Jesus delivers; St. Paul warns us that the air we breathe is full of these invisible spirits; in the Apocalypse an angel is seen to descend from heaven and bind the old serpent for a time, during which he can no longer seduce the nations, after which he is to be unbound, etc.

Profane histories, in their turn, are all filled with prodigies wrought by the gods of Paganism, who were no other than the devils. Certain abridgments of the classics represent these narratives as mere popular legends; but open the ancient authors themselves, and you will there see that all history must either be called in question, or the reality of these marvellous facts be doubted, facts which are more than ever unaccountable to the unbeliever at a time when the laws of nature have been so much studied; very easily understood when, with the Church and mankind, we know that spirits, as well as man, and *more than man*, effect, by their will, changes and modifications in the material world.

V.

ARE THE EVIL SPIRITS RESPONSIBLE FOR
ALL THE MISCHIEF ASCRIBED TO THEM?

Not always. A drunkard swears that
the Devil appeared to him, spoke to him,
struck him. In reality, the Devil simply
reminded him of the tavern; the fumes
of the liquor did the rest. A rascal,
cleverly availing himself of the credulity
of simpletons, gets up for himself the
reputation of being a sorcerer, and boasts
of having the Devil for his colleague,
makes his clients pay for consultations
with which Satan has nothing to do—
every day our courts of justice condemn
such tricks, and exculpate the Devil from
a chimerical complicity. But whence
comes it that people can, with some
truth, attribute to the Devil mischief of
which he is not the author?—From his
bad reputation, most authentically estab-
lished.

Humanity, expelled from the terrestrial paradise, under the weight of a condemnation the most terrible; then drowned in the waters of the Deluge; then plunged, with the exception of one small nation divinely protected, into the darkness and abominations of idolatry; the Word made flesh, crucified; the blood of ten millions shed; the benign mission of the Church constantly obstructed by schisms, heresies, persecutions, and calumnies — there is a very incomplete abridgment of the incontestible works of the evil spirits in the moral and religious order.

In the material order, diabolical action, like that of God and the good angels, is generally veiled under the appearance of events purely natural. The lightning that struck the house in which the children of Job were assembled seemed a purely physical effect; the Holy Scripture teaches us that this time Satan himself directed the electric fluid. One day

St. Francis de Sales was blessing a church-yard; a torrent of rain prevented the ceremony. The saint, who was in no wise faint-hearted, made an exorcism, and immediately the firmament recovered its serenity. Men have always been convinced that a host of calamities which occur in the world are not mere fortuitous combinations of the physical laws which govern matter. They believe in the "indignation, and wrath, and trouble which he sends by evil angels," (Ps. LXXVII, 49;) and, without neglecting physical means of struggling against pestilence and famine, they have recourse to prayer, and events have often proved that this weapon is the most powerful. Many times, after a procession in honor of the Blessed Virgin, a consecration to the Sacred Heart of Jesus, the plague suddenly ceases. The materialist sees in this only a chance coincidence; popular sense sees differently, and it is not mistaken.

"It is an impiety," says the learned Gerson, "and an error directly contrary to Holy Writ, to deny that the devils are the authors of many surprising effects. Those who regard what is told of this as a fable would deserve severe reprehension. . . . Sometimes, even learned men are prone to this error, because they allow their faith to be weakened and the natural lights to be obscured. Their soul, wholly occupied with sensible things, refers all to the body, and cannot raise itself to the spiritual." (*De error, circà art. mag.*)

Must it be said? The Christians of our times have been subjected to the materialistic atmosphere in which they live. Without denying diabolical agency, in principle, they are always disposed to deny it in fact. To hear them, one would imagine that, fatigued with sixty centuries of mischievous activity, Satan had really turned hermit. Thus, when, some years ago, it was noised about that the venerable Curé d'Ars had to undergo the external assaults of the invisible enemy, who would believe it? Many ecclesiastics laughed, like the vulgar, at these supposed devilish tricks! But what happened one day? It was at St. Trivier, where a mission was going on. During supper, there was a learned dissertation on the fancies of the good curé, who eat too little, slept badly, and took the rats for the Devil. But, behold! at midnight they are all suddenly awoke by a fearful uproar; the house is all in confusion; the doors bang, the windows shiver, the walls totter, and seem, by their crackling noise, as though they were going to fall! In a moment every one is up. They remember that the Curé d'Ars has said, "You will not be surprised if you chance to hear some noise to-night." They rush to his room; he is sound asleep. "Get up," they cry, "the presbytery is going to fall!" "Oh, I know well what it is," he replies, smiling; "you must go to bed; there is nothing to fear." (See his *Life*, by Monnin.) Next day, no one laughed at M. Vianney.

Habitually more hidden, and for that reason more perfidious, diabolical agency is but too real; and if humanity were left unaided, it would long ago have been crushed in an unequal contest.

VI.

BUT WHAT INTEREST HAS THE DEVIL IN INJURING US?

The interest of his malice, his envy, his hatred!

1. It is a general law of creation that each superior being attracts and assimilates to itself the inferior being. Inorganic matter is attracted by vegetable matter, vegetable by animal, all three by man, man by the angel. Less sensible to him who can see only with the eyes of the body, this superior form of the gen-

eral law is not less real than the others; the angel, even fallen, still attracts man; but he attracts him according to the actual dispositions of his perverted will, to make him bad, as he has himself become.

2. The conduct of bad men helps us, alas! to understand that of the Devil. They walk in the ways of darkness; they rejoice when they have done evil, and they take delight in wicked actions. Devoured by the want of acting, and no longer able to share with man the grace, the joy, the purity he has lost, the Devil tries to inoculate him with impiety, blasphemy, aversion to the Supreme Good. He sees the faithful angel, after having conquered in the great struggle between the two angelic armies, accomplishing for man, his young brother, the charitable ministry which has been confided to him; he sees man, overwhelmed with those magnificent gifts of which he is ignominiously despoiled, ascending towards the

throne which his fall left vacant. He is jealous, and his jealousy urges him unceasingly, with sin and by sin, to make death reign on earth. In short, powerless to strike God, whose arm chastises his insolence, he tries to avenge himself on the weaker beings whom God surrounds with His paternal tenderness. The Apostle St. John tells us so in brief but luminous terms:

"There was a great battle in heaven. Michael and his angels fought with the dragon; and the dragon fought, and his angels. And they prevailed not; neither was their place found any more in heaven. And that great dragon was cast out, the old serpent, who is called the Devil, and Satan, who seduceth the whole world: and he was cast forth unto the earth; and his angels were thrown down with him. . . . Woe to the earth and to the sea, because the Devil is come down unto you, having great wrath, knowing that he hath but a short time. And after the dragon saw that he was cast unto the earth, he persecuted the woman who brought forth the man-child, [*the mysterious woman whom the prophet sees clothed with the sun, Mary :*] and there were given to the woman two wings, [*to escape him ;*] . . . and the dragon was angry against the woman, and went to make war with the rest of her seed, which keep the commandments of God, and have the testimony of Jesus Christ." (Apoc., XII.)

Undoubtedly, in this war the Devil will finally gain only an increase of rage and confusion at sight of the Blessed, who, in such great numbers, shall have conquered him, and whose glory and happiness his vain attacks shall enhance ; but *now*, he satisfies his malice, he creates an empire for himself, he thwarts the designs of his conqueror. This is enough to make him that "roaring lion who goeth about seeking whom he may devour." (I Peter, v, 8.)

VII.

THE RELIGION OF THE DEVIL.

To speak of *religion* is to speak of the bond which unites and binds man to God, in the first place, and, afterwards, to God's other creatures, according to their nature and their place in the general plan of the universe. To adore God; to honor good spirits and virtuous men, whom God, as a good Father, makes partakers of his beneficent power; to practice justice and charity towards his fellow-creatures, and to make the material world a means of perfection for man, and not an obstacle to the reign of God—such are the marks of the true religion. * False religions fail in one or more of these four fundamental conditions, either by excess or omission. Thus Protestantism, which gives no honor to the angels and saints, sins by omission. Assuredly, it does none too much for God;

---

*For since none but the true religion can be from God, all other religions must be from the father of lies; and therefore highly displeasing to the God of truth. (St. Matthew 24:5, 24) but it should do more for God's friends. A certain Norman sailor, having been cast, in a storm, on the English coast, being very ill, he received a visit from the Protestant minister. At first they agreed wonderfully well; the minister talked to him of our Saviour's charity, and the sailor found that, with the exception of the costume, the minister replaced his priest very well. However, he interrupted him, saying, "But you do not speak to me of the Blessed Virgin!" "No, we do not care about Mary." "You do not care about Mary! You do not honor the Blessed Virgin, Mother of God! Well, you are not a true priest of the true religion!" And the old sailor sent the minister to—all the devils.

On this last point his zeal was intemperate, but fundamentally he was right. Since the preaching of the Gospel, religions which formed themselves by separation from Catholicity, the universal religion, sin, in general, by omission.

They do not wish to submit on such or such a point; if it be a dogma, they deny it; if it be a commandment, they forget it. That makes, according to the saying of a worthy workman, at his last hour, religions "very convenient for *living*, but not at all for *dying*." Not daring to do more, the Devil contents himself with preventing heretics and schismatics from serving God as He deserves to be served.

Where the splendid light of the Gospel requires no circumspection, the Devil, more audacious, demands a sacrilegious worship. Idolatry, which covered nearly the whole earth from the Deluge to the coming of Christ, and reigns still in immense countries, consists in this double crime : rendering to created spirits the worship of *adoration*, due to God alone, and rendering that worship to *evil spirits*, through fear, interest, or human respect.

The authors of many books giving minute details on the religions of antiquity, might have avoided blunders, if

they had known how to read in the
Psalmist that clear and precise affirma-
tion, "ALL THE GODS OF THE GENTILES
ARE DEVILS," (Ps. xcv;) and in St. Paul,
who had a near view of Paganism still
living and master of the world: "The
things which the heathens sacrifice, they
sacrifice to devils, and not to God."
(I Cor., x.) So that Paganism is the
religion of the Devil, nothing else.

One is amazed—and no wonder—to
see men who were not struck with mental
aberration, prostrate themselves before
carved wood and stone, before the stars
of the firmament, and even before vile
animals; but a more serious and profound study of Paganism has shown that,
in general, Pagans did not adore their
statues any more than we do ours; they
adored the spirits which they believed to
reside in those statues, in those stars, in
those animals, spirits which, often, gave
proofs of their power.

The first of theologians, and the most

profound of philosophers, St. Thomas, has given the true explanation of Paganism in these few words : " Man might be *in part* the cause of idolatry, by the disorder of his affections, by the pleasure he found in symbolical representations, and by his ignorance. But the fundamental cause (*consummativa*) must be sought in the devils, who cause men to adore them under the form of idols, *therein working certain things which excited their wonder and admiration.*" (S. Th., II, II, 94.)

Nearer than we to the cradle of the world, and better instructed in primitive facts, the ancient nations knew perfectly well that spirits exercised a continual agency in the universe. The materialistic philosophy, which attributes all external phenomena to laws constantly and everywhere blind, and boldly denies that any spirit whatsoever could ever interfere in the distribution of *rain and fine weather*, is an error comparatively recent.

On the other hand, to obtain from us the homage they no longer merit, and the adoration which is due to God alone, is the constant ambition of the angels of the abyss. Let us open the Gospel. The Devil approaches Jesus, whom he does not yet know, but whose holiness disturbs and irritates him, trying to urge him to an act of pride, then to an act of presumption; and, finally, showing him the kingdoms of the world, and all the glory thereof, tells him, "All this will I give to thee, if, falling down, thou wilt adore me!" Behold the depth of the Devil's thought, to be adored. (And they are like unto him who, in the delirium of their shameful passions, are willing to forget their Creator's right, and say to them, "I adore thee!") Satan, that *ape of God*, as he is called by the Fathers, pretends to reign in His place, at least over a portion of mankind. By a just and terrible judgment, God has left men free to choose their own master, and the

Devil, fostering their passions, to deceive them, has altars raised to himself, which the Cross alone could miraculously overthrow.

Finally, to adore one's self is a learned folly which cannot become popular. The nations adore either a Supreme Spirit, or *spirits* whose power, limited undoubtedly, yet superior to ours, dazzles them.

VIII.

CAN A RATIONAL MAN BELIEVE NOW IN SORCERY?

This question of sorcery is very grave. It involves the external and visible agency of our invisible foes. All mankind has believed, from the most remote ages, in the existence of sorcery. Antiquity called it *magic*, a word which, sometimes, signifies merely superior learning, like that of the three kings who came to Bethlehem to adore Our Lord—magi kings, but not magicians. The name of *théurgie* was given to the invocation of spirits supposed to be beneficent, and that of *goétie* to the having recourse to wicked spirits to obtain the success of criminal designs.

The Bible does not confine itself to declaring that the object of idolatrous worship is the devils; it signalizes and condemns in almost every page the real and criminal relations of the idolaters with their gods, with those "strange gods . . . that were newly gotten up, whom their fathers worshipped not." (Deut. xxxii, 16, 17.)

Achab refuses to hear Micheas. Micheas tells him, "There came forth a spirit, and stood before the Lord, and said: 'I will deceive him.' And the Lord said to him: 'By what means?' And he said: 'I will go forth, and be a lying spirit in the mouth of all his prophets.' And the Lord said to him: 'Thou shalt deceive him, and shalt prevail; go forth, and do so.'" "Now, therefore," continues Micheas, "behold the Lord hath given *a lying spirit* in the mouth of all thy prophets, . . . and the Lord hath spoken evil against thee." (III Kings, XXII.)

So Achab dies, and his son Ochozias succeeds him. Dangerously ill in his turn, the new king sends to ask Beelzebub, the god of Accaron, whether he is to recover from his illness.

Then the angel of the Lord sends Elias, the prophet, to meet his messengers, and he says to them : "Is there not a God in Israel, that ye go to consult Beelzebub, the god of Accaron ? Wherefore, go tell the king, thy master, thus sayeth the Lord : 'From the bed on which thou art gone up, thou shalt not come down, but thou shalt surely die.' . . . So he died, according to the word of the Lord which Elias spake." (IV Kings, chap. I.) Hard lesson for those who think it allowable to consult, *only in case of illness*, as they say, modern oracles, so perfectly identical with those of old!

But let us hear a touching story related in the Third Book of Kings. Elias, the prophet of the true God, presenting himself before Achab, demands that he shall gather together all the people, as also all his false prophets, on Mount Carmel. When all were assembled, the prophet of God said: "How long do you halt between two sides? If the Lord be God, follow him; but if Baal, then follow him." And the people did not answer him a word. And Elias said again to the people: "I only remain a prophet of the Lord; but the prophets of Baal are four hundred and fifty men. Let two bullocks be given us, and let them choose one bullock for themselves, and cut it in pieces, and lay it upon wood, but put no fire under; and I will dress the other bullock, and lay it on wood, and put no fire under it. Call ye on the names of your gods, and I will call on the name of my Lord."

Specially enlightened from above, Elias counts on a miracle; but the false prophets are not frightened. They know that the Devil habitually aids them in their magical operations; they agree, therefore, to a public test, the consequences of which will be dreadful, in case of failure. So when they had placed the victim on the wood, they began to call on Baal, and to dance around their altars; but no answer came, no fire to kindle the wood. Elias said jestingly to them: "Cry with a louder voice, for he is a god; and, perhaps, he is talking, or is in an inn, or on a journey; or perhaps he is asleep." New incantations were tried, and great magical expedients. They make, according to the custom of their idolatrous rites, incisions in their flesh with knives and lancets; their blood flows in streams. But the power of the Devil is still controlled by a superior power. Elias acts in his turn. He immolates the victim, places it on the altar, over which he had caused several buckets of water to be thrown; then he prays, and suddenly, before all the people, fire from heaven consumes the holocaust, the wood, the stones, the dust, even, and the water that was in the trench. (III Kings, XVIII.)

By the prophet's orders the four hundred and fifty priests of Baal were put to death. Protected by the impious Achab, the sworn enemy of Elias, and fed at the table of Jezabel, the queen, these seducers would have known how to defend themselves, if the miracle wrought by the prophet of the true God had not been a crushing evidence.

The apostolic times present, in their turn, the best authenticated acts of sorcery. St. Paul found at Salamis, in the house of the pro-consul, Sergius Paulus, a magician named Elymas. The Apostle did not say to the pro-consul, as certain

enlightened men of modern times would
have said, "This wretch is only a juggler." Filled with the Holy Ghost, *reple-
tus Spiritu Sancto*, he looks upon him,
calls him "son of the Devil," and in the
name of the Lord, strikes him with blindness. (Acts, XIII.) Another day, in the
town of Philippi, Paul met a young girl
who had a divining spirit, (*spiritum
pythonis*,) and by reason thereof gained
much money for her masters. The Apostle commanded the spirit to depart; the
sorceress became, thenceforth, powerless
to continue her trade. The consequence
was the indignation of her masters and a
popular tumult. (Acts, XVI.)

But a drama, too little studied, is the
struggle between St. Peter, the founder
of the Church, and Simon, the magician.
This Simon, who bore the same name
that Peter had before his call, appears at
the beginning of Christianity as the chief
representative of the infernal powers,
who, vanquished on Calvary, were bound

to continue to the end the contest against the society divinely founded, but could never prevail. The learned may find, in the Annals of Baronius, an enumeration of grave authors, both Pagan and Christian, who relate the facts of which we can here give only a summary.

The preaching of the Gospel was scarcely commenced, when Simon recognizes in the wonders wrought by the fishermen of Genezareth, a power superior to that of the devils. Immediately he hastens to offer the Apostles a sum of money, probably considerable, to enable him also, by the imposition of hands, to communicate the Holy Ghost. (Doubtless, he gave himself little concern about communicating *holiness ;* he had in view only the extraordinary gifts which then frequently accompanied confirmation.) The apostles indignantly repulsed him, and exhorted him to do penance. Far from heeding these useful and charitable counsels, Simon is hardened, and, profiting by the hatred of the Jews for the Apostles, he calls himself the Power of God, and pretends to have come down as *Father* amongst the Samaritans, as *Son* amongst the Jews, and to go to other nations as the Holy Ghost.

Immorality is the usual companion of impiety; the magician brings with him a woman bought in a bad house, in Tyre, and presents her as the first conception of his spirit, and the mother of all creation. In Pagan countries the imposter says nothing of the Father, Son, or Holy Ghost; he causes himself to be worshipped as Jupiter; Helen, his concubine, is Minerva; and the priests of the god and goddess honor them both by practices of magic and habits of debauchery.

Simon Peter, vicar of Jesus Christ, and Simon Jupiter, first-born of Satan, according to St. Irenæus, meet at Rome, under Nero, Simon Peter amongst the poor whom he is evangelizing, Simon

Jupiter at the court of the Emperor, passionately devoted to magic, and desirous, says Pliny, of succeeding by that black art in commanding the gods themselves.

The magician promises to fly in the air in the amphitheatre, before all the people. On the day appointed, he actually does fulfil his promise, and, ascends, borne up invisibly by devils, amid the acclamations of the multitude. But a man in the crowd below kneels and prays; it is Simon Peter. The prayer of the Apostle ascends to the throne of God; the vanquished devils cease to bear up their accomplice, who falls to the ground and breaks his legs. His blood besprinkles even the Emperor, and he dies impenitent two days after. The people, witnessing this terrible scene, begin to believe in the power of the Crucified, whom Simon Peter publicly invoked. It is true Simon Peter shall die, in his turn, on the cross; but his death shall be for the Church he founds the beginning of an endless reign.

The first ages of the Church reproduce, under a thousand forms, and in all places, this first contest and this first triumph. The Fathers, in their discussions with Pagans, do not say: "Your Paganism is only a cheat, an imposture!" They know, often by their personal experience, that the devils manifest themselves by FACTS. (Arnobus, for example, before his conversion, interrogated enchanted amulets, which gave him answers as intelligible as those of the tables to our modern spiritualists; furthermore, *spoken answers!*) The Fathers say to the nations: "Behold, the power of your demons everywhere yields to the power of Christ. Hence, Christ is the conqueror, and the only Master who must be served."

Magic survives the ruin of Paganism as a public worship. Proscribed and forced to hide itself, the traffic with devils assumes a more and more malevolent character. Civil, as well as religious laws, punish it with severity, yet do not succeed in abolishing it. It is, in fact, one of those plagues the germs of which are always in existence. Ever will the evil spirits be ready to offer services for which they shall one day make people pay dear; ever will rampant human passions go the length even of making compact with the enemy, provided they are immediately satisfied.

We can neither, then, in this little work, adduce the testimonies of all profane historians, agreeing with those of all the Fathers, nor sketch the history of sorcery from the beginning of Christianity to our days.

Two remarks only are here necessary.

1. The palmy time of sorcery was not at all in the Middle Ages, but in the enlightened age of the Revival and the Reformation. England, after becoming Protestant, burned witches and wizards

by thousands; her most authentic historians record the fact.

2. The process used by the magistracy against sorcerers consisted not, as has been said either wickedly or foolishly, in subjecting the accused to tortures, amid which they confessed anything and everything. The magistrates of the Middle Ages and of the first part of modern times were neither idiots, nor bloodsuckers. They began by investigating the affair according to the common rules of law proceedings, and when proof was made, that is to say, when the accused was found guilty, *then*, according to the custom of the time, he or she might be put to the torture, to obtain either confession, which seemed a necessary reparation, or the discovery of the accomplices. That there were abuses in these matters is very certain; but such was the rule. As to the real guilt of the condemned, it results, amongst other things, from the calm and serious confession

made, in the moment of torture, by a great number of sorcerers who were not ignorant that this confession was of no human advantage to them. M. Bizouard, who has studied the accounts of many of these trials, makes the judicious remark that, the oldest and most guilty usually died in despair, whereas the younger and less culpable asked pardon of God and man, and died penitent.

Cases of sorcery have become more rare during these last two centuries. We have stated the reason. The wind was setting towards materialism, and the evil spirit seemed to be dead.

IX.

CAN A NATURAL EXPLANATION BE GIVEN OF FACTS SUPPOSED TO BE DIABOLICAL?

Sometimes, doubtless, but not always. Long before our "philosophers," Daniel caught the priests of Bel in the act of imposture.

King Nabuchodonosor said to the young Israelite who refused to prostrate himself before the idol: "Why dost thou not adore Bel? Thinkest thou he is not a living God? Seest thou not how much he eats and drinks every day?" Daniel smiled and said: "O king, be not deceived, for this Bel is but clay within and brass without; neither hath he eaten at any time." The king, being angry, called for his priests, and said to them: "If you tell me not who it is that eateth up these expenses, you shall die. But if you can show that Bel eateth these things, Daniel shall die, because he hath blasphemed against Bel." And Daniel said to the king: "Be it done according to thy word." Now the priests of Bel were seventy, besides their wives and children. And the king went with Daniel into the temple of Bel. And the priests of Bel said: "Behold, we go out; and do thou, O king, set on the meats, and make ready the wine, and shut the

door fast, and seal it with thy own ring."
The king then causes to be brought the
usual provision of the god, twelve great
measures of fine flour, forty sheep, and
sixty vessels of wine. This god was not
a small eater! Daniel, on his side,
strews the pavement with an imperceptible layer of ashes. The morrow came;
the seal is found unbroken, the doors
are opened. The table of the god is
empty!!! "Great art thou, O Bel,"
cried the king. Daniel laughed: "Behold this pavement; mark whose foot-
steps these are." The priests of the idols
had come during the night, with their
families, to sup in place of the god and
at the expense of his credulous worshippers. (Daniel, XIV.)

Many reasons explain the considerable
share which imposture often had in operations considered as magical. The power
of the devils is in itself limited, and, on
the other hand, they do not communicate
it with boundless liberality. The state

of theurgist, magician, sorcerer, magnetizer, "medium," confederate of Satan,
appears to many lucrative and advantageous; many, neither knowing how, nor
daring, nor being able to hold intercourse
with spirits, have had recourse to jugglery. Imposture is frequently manifested in the works of the last defenders
of Paganism when it was giving way
before the Gospel. The oracles were
silent; they made oracles. Prodigies
ceased; they feigned to work prodigies.
Precisely because the nations had been
accustomed to superhuman proofs of
the reality and power of spirits, it was
felt that the cause of Paganism was
lost, if diabolical wonders disappeared
from the scene before evangelical miracles.

Recourse was then had to skilful imposture; the famous Life of *Apollonius*
of Thyane, a set-off for the Man-God,
was everywhere circulated; the physical
sciences, then somewhat advanced, were

employed to counterfeit what was no longer to be done.

When an unscrupulous man has no more good money, he issues bad; the latter is taken, because the value of the former was recognized. The true reason why pretended sorcerers so easily find dupes, is that there have been, and still are, real sorcerers. The more Christian a country is, the rarer they are. Hence it is that M. Mullois could say to his French readers: "A sorcerer is a rascal, and he that listens to him is a fool." Hence it is that our card-drawers and fortune-tellers are only swindlers employed in shearing a flock of simpletons. But in China, even now, as testified by our holiest missionaries, magical influences are so active that *two thousand Pagans*, on an average, in the course of the year, have themselves baptized to escape the external power of the devils.

In the seventeenth century Fontenelle wrote a *History of Oracles*, an ingenious, but rather superficial dissertation, in which the superhuman events of Paganism were humanly explained. Father Baltus replied so judiciously that Fontenelle, a man of mind and taste as he was, left his book there, and said that Father Baltus had *converted him to the Devil!* In our own days, anti-Christian authors, proud of a small stock of erudition, with some tincture of physics, have altered the groundwork of Fontenelle's thesis by extending it to the Divine supernatural itself. Have we not seen, as it were yesterday, an audacious Atheist transform into tricks of jugglery the very miracles of the Gospel? Thousands of men fed in the desert with five loaves; the waves of the sea suddenly calmed; multitudes of the sick, the blind, the deaf, the lame, paralytics, lepers, etc., instantaneously cured, some in distant places; the dead themselves raised before a whole people, before the learned of that time, infuriate enemies of Christ—

all that, thanks to a certain scientific jargon very fit to convince *idlers*—all that is explained NATURALLY!

Brave philosophers! They prove to a certainty that they are not sorcerers! But if they will only condescend so far as to open their eyes and look at what is being done, even at this day, by spiritism, they will see that communication with spirits is not a fable, but, alas, a fearful reality!

X.

WHAT IS A CONTRACT WITH THE DEVIL?

It is a contract by virtue of which the Devil grants to man a certain share of his power, in consideration of a price which he demands, and which is usually the renunciation of eternal salvation. Here we must distinguish, with St. Thomas, between the *express* contract and that which is *implicit*, or *understood*. When the Devil is invoked, appears under a visible form, converses with the unfortunate being who has called upon him, discusses with him the conditions of his unhallowed favors, and receives in return a promise of obedience, an abjuration of baptism, there is an express contract.

The contract is implicit when, with the legitimate suspicion that Satan is playing a part in certain mysterious practices, such as divers modes of incantation by the wand, by cards, by table-turning, recourse is still had to those practices.

It is evident that a contract with the Devil is an enormous crime. Certain authors, even Catholic authors, seem to believe it impossible. If, instead of theorizing at their desk, they would question the pastors of our rural districts, they would tell them that these abominable doings are still going on; they would tell them that *sorcerers*, touched by grace, have confessed, on beginning a new life, the reality of these contracts, which they had signed with their blood.

Some crazy individuals think themselves possessed; others imagine that they have made such contracts; just as certain other lunatics fancy themselves emperors or gods; but all the predecessors of Simon the Magician and his whole race cannot be considered as insane.

St. Augustine (*De div. quæs.*, 79) formally attributes the prodigies wrought by magicians to "contracts" properly so called—*magi faciunt miracula per privatos contractus*—and he explains why the devils, desirous of being honored, show themselves faithful to their promises. He adds that if, in the sacrilegious rites of the worship of evil spirits, the holy name of God is found mixed up, the success of the operation is not on that account a grace from on high, but rather a terrible punishment. For this is the way of blindness and of hardness. An observation which we recommend to the apologists of superstitious practices, which cannot be criminal, they maintain, since they are mingled with pious prayers and blessed objects.

The compact with Satan, more horrible in Christians, since it then includes a formal renunciation of Our Saviour Jesus Christ, is more frequent amongst infidels, where it is often the very foundation of idolatry.

Amongst numerous examples of anti-baptism, in the state of general custom, we shall cite "nagualism," (*nahual*, genius, familiar devil.) Missionaries found a strange superstition prevailing all over Mexico. Before admitting a postulant to initiation (when he had been a Christian) the nagualist master makes him renounce the Saviour, and curse the invocation of the Virgin and the Saints. He afterwards washed the head and the different parts of the body where he had received the baptismal unction, in order, he said, to efface all traces thereof. The child was dedicated to the *visible or invisible pro-*

tector of his whole life. The master then opened a vein behind the ear, or under the tongue, drew thence some drops of blood, and offered it to the Devil, in token of the compact which the child contracted with his *nagual*. Before leaving him, the master named to the father the forest or the cavern to which, at the age of reason, the child was to repair in order to ratify, in person, with his nagual, the contract entered into in his name. (Paris *Moniteur*, March 16 and 17, 1854.) Afterwards, the youth repaired to the place appointed, and, amid the horror of the night, offered sacrifice to the demon, who caused his nagual to appear under the form of the animal whose name he bore, and who then showed himself gentle and caressing. This interview is, as it were, the seal of the compact made with the Devil.

XI.

HAS THE DEVIL GOAT'S FEET AND HORNS?

Having no body, the Devil has neither feet nor horns of any kind. If, with God's permission, he enters into direct communication with man, he must have recourse, like the good angels themselves, to a visible form.

Probably all forms are not permitted to him.

The corporal form is the natural image of the moral state. If, amongst us now, beauty and vice, virtue and ugliness are often enough united, that is but a provisional consequence of the state of trial. The blessed will shine eternally with a beauty proportionate to the splendor of their virtues; the ugliness of the damned will be proportionate to the greatness of their crimes. When the good angels appear to men, it is under a majestic and graceful form.

Satan lost his beauty with his justice. He is moral ugliness itself. We may conceive that his Judge and Master, when He allows him to show himself visibly, compels him to wear habitually a corporal form which reveals his moral degradation. The goat being, in the grand scene of the Last Judgment, the symbol of the slaves of sin, there is nothing to prevent us from admitting that the Devil may sometimes have shown himself under that form, or some other similar one. In Eden he bore that of a serpent; and the history of several saints shows him under the human form, debased by the expression of vice, a form more ignominious still than that of the animals.

St. Stanislaus Kotska and the venerable Curé of Ars saw him in the form of a dog, which is the symbol of the shameless vice. In certain circumstances, he may take temporary possession of the body of a real animal, and make it the instrument of his illusions. This is the most natural explanation of the worship of animals, such as sacred serpents, the ox, apis, etc. The devils wrought in animals the same prodigies as in statues.

St. Paul warns us that Satan can transform himself into an angel of light, and we read of his assuming the appearance of holy personages, the better to seduce, as, on occasion, he speaks in devout language the better to persuade. Against an enemy so artful the infallible light of the Church is very necessary.

But this question of the several forms which the devil may assume has nothing to do with faith. What is certain is, that the worshippers of the Devil have often represented him under the form of a goat or some other hideous figure. We may be convinced of this by seeing the oriental idols in our museums. To us, these are frightful and grotesque figures; to the idolaters by whom they were fabricated, these statues were the dwelling and the image of their divinities! Divinities deformed, unshapely, without beauty or harmony; unquiet powers, *fallen angels !*

Christian artists are not the inventors of this symbolism, nevertheless they have very judiciously adopted it. To those embellishers of Satan who give to the vices of which he is the father an enchanting appearance, they are true to the part they play : Catholic art has another, more salutary and more true.

XII.

IS THE DEVIL A PROPHET ?

God alone knows future events that depend on free causes. For instance, what shall be done and what willed by some one who shall only be born many ages hence ? He alone, for instance, could dictate to the sacred writers, more than eight hundred years in advance, the most minute and the most precise details concerning the acts of our Lord Jesus Christ.

But the Devil may know what our eye perceiveth not, and what is passing in a place very far away. A pure spirit, not subjected, as we are, to know only through the medium of corporal organs, sees more things at once, and sees deeper than we do. He may, besides, thanks to his potent intelligence and his long experience, draw better than we from the present what he knows, by conjecture, of the future. Finally, he may announce things that he counts on accomplishing himself, or having accomplished by those who willingly receive his inspiration. This explains the justice of certain answers given by the oracles of the Pagans. These oracles, be it remembered, always played an immense part in private and in public life, amongst idolatrous nations, ancient and modern. They not only consulted them on the future, but specially asked advice from them, which advice was followed with blind confidence. Some skeptics may have, doubtless, scoffed at the omens, as other unbelievers now scoff at even the Divine prophecies of the Gospel; but these were exceptions, and the evil spirits, by their oracles, ruled Greece and Rome, as they still, by similar means, rule Guinea and Congo.

The most famous oracle was that of Delphi. Cresus, king of Lydia, as Herodotus relates, wanted, one day, to put it to the trial, before asking its advice. Deputies set out from Sardes, with orders to ask the oracle, the hundredth day after their departure, what their king was doing that day. The priestess of Apollo answers them : "My senses are struck with the smell of a turtle, which is being cooked with lamb's flesh in a brazen cauldron, the cover of which is also of brass." Cresus himself had actually cut up a turtle and a lamb, and had them cooked in a brazen vessel! Seeing at a distance was practiced before Mesmer and the modern magnetizers. Other facts show the Devil having recourse to gasconade, when the future puzzles him. Being consulted by Pyrrhus, who was thinking of attacking the Romans, the oracle answers: "I say thou the Romans can beat;"[*] which likewise signifies: "I say the Romans can beat thee." With this wretched play on words, the oracle was sure to be always right.

Very often, those spirits of darkness gave, either through ignorance or malice, answers that were absolutely false, as we see by the passage from Micheas, quoted hereafter. Sometimes, but very rarely, God compelled them, or their slaves, to proclaim the truth. This is seen by the story of Balaam. Balaam was a magician sold to the devils; brought by King Balak, the enemy of the people of Israel, in sight of the camp of the Hebrews, to curse them, he prophesies the mysterious

[*] Aio te, Æacide, Romanos vincere posse.

Star which was to rise from Jacob on the world.

Every one knows that the bloody sacrifice of the Redeeming God marked the end of the reign of oracles. They became silent. But how? Was it because, *at last*, some ingenious philosophers had discovered the fraud of the interpreters of the gods, just as our tribunals of to-day discover the imposture of so-called sorcerers? Not at all. But at the moment when *human interest* more than ever urged them to speak, they were silent. The idolaters of those days well knew the cause of that silence. "What wonder," cries the famous Pagan philosopher Porphyrus, "that Rome has been for so many years ravaged by the plague? Esculapius and the other gods have left it; for, since Jesus is adored, no one obtains any more the public assistance of the gods." "And when," remarks the learned author of *Paganism, its Origin, its History*, "when is this complaint heard? In the third century, in all the fire of persecution, under the rule of the Pagan Cesars, priests, and gods, when no human power could enchain the divinities of Olympus nor close the mouth of the oracles."

In this great conflict of the infant Church, it must be understood that men, on either side, did not struggle alone; Christ and His faithful angels assisted the martyrs, Satan and his angels multiplied their spells to complete the blindness of the executioners. The cessation of the oracles, and the public confessions to which the Christians forced the devils, were amongst the principal means of the *supernatural triumph* of the Cross.

Now-a-days the oracles of fortune-tellers, *clairvoyantes*, and table-turners have little public renown; governments do not submit to them questions of peace or war; but let the Christian faith grow weak or die out, and we shall again see the days when the nations took for their guides the demons of Delphi, of Dodona, and Prenesta. Rationalistic pride is soon at an end; humanity feels the want of a superior guidance; take from it the Gospel and the Church, and it will to-morrow question the devils. Either Divine faith, or diabolical superstitions.

XIII.

IS THE DEVIL A DOCTOR?

If, to make a physician, these three things were required: learning, skill, devotion—Satan never was a doctor. We do not dispute his learning and skill, but he absolutely lacks devotion.

Nevertheless, that deceitful master, knowing the value that men set on health, and their dislike of suffering and death, contrived, in all ages, to pass himself off as a potent and generous healer. The ancients, even to Hippocrates, knew no other physicians than the Pagan priests, who ascribed to their knowledge

a superhuman origin, and to their medi-
caments a superhuman virtue. The creation of natural medicine no wise discon-
certed them, and magic remedies are in
use even in our own days.

There are five distinct sorts of remedies that may be employed against a
disease : 1. *Natural remedies*, prepared
by medical art, and to which recourse is
habitually had.   2. *Remedies the prepara-
tion of which is the secret* of a family or
an individual, but in the composition of
which superstition has no share : recourse may be had to such when experience has proved them not unsafe.   Still
it is wise to consult a medical man,
because a medicine that suited one sick
person might be injurious to another.
3. *Supernatural remedies* of the right
kind, such as the invocation of the
friends of God, the application of their
relics, pilgrimages to their tomb ; provided one does not believe that these
acts will produce, necessarily, and of

themselves, the cure. Even though the
confidence of the pilgrims were false,
they would in no wise sin; for what they
do, they do to obtain from Almighty
God, through the intercession of a saint,
that he may grant the cure. 4. *Superstitious remedies,* in the making up, and use
of which are introduced either the direct
invocation of the Devil, or fantastic ceremonies, a sort of sacramental formula
of magic, or the prayers of the Church
employed otherwise than the Church
prescribes, and thereby profaned. 5.
Finally, *pretended superstitious remedies,*
sold as such by false sorcerers to the
fools whom they can cheat. As these
false sorcerers have, usually, no medical knowledge, their drugs, which never
cure, almost always aggravate the disease, if they do not kill the patient.

Large allowance being made for quackery, we may acknowledge, with St. Augustine and other illustrious personages
that, in certain cases, cures are effected

by diabolical agency. In the opinion of several Fathers, the devils usually confine themselves to removing causes of suffering to which they themselves gave rise. "They wound," says Tertullian, "they cease to wound, people think they have cured!" However that may be, it is always a crime to have recourse to the enemy of God to get rid of a cross which His providence imposes; and, without speaking of the risk, serious as it is, of being tricked by a swindler whose drugs may *endanger life itself*, it is always a double folly: first, because God, being ever the strongest, may well strike us, in spite of the assistance of the Devil, sacrilegiously invoked; second, because the Devil, who hates us, will make us pay *very dear* for his consultations and the momentary relief his power may have procured.

If you are sick, call in a regular physician, and pray God to make the remedies he prescribes efficacious.

XIV.

ON THE PRESENT COMMUNICATIONS WITH EVIL SPIRITS, OR SPIRITUALISM.

In the latter years of the eighteenth century, a period of scoffing incredulity which affected to believe "neither in God nor Devil," there appeared a certain Mesmer, who, by means of certain passes, plunged people into a sleep, accompanied by very singular circumstances. To the German physician Mesmer, succeeded the Italian swindler Balsamo, styled, in France, Count de Cagliostro, or *the divine Cagliostro*, for that adventurer, after decamping in all haste from Rome, where the galleys awaited him, infatuated the philosophical society of Paris to a degree that exceeds all belief. "His hair," says Bresciani, "was encased in precious jewels; people kept, as a treasure, a pinch of his toilet powder; his portraits were everywhere; Cagliostro was painted on fans, and stamped on handkerchiefs; he was cast in bronze, and statues were raised to him as to a tutelary god." But what! Balsamo, finding the forging of notes insufficient for his activity, was, moreover, Grand Master of Egyptian Freemasonry, and heir of Mesmer's science. His somnambulists brought, before wondering materialists, the forgotten spells of ancient magic; like the priestesses of Delphi, they announced the future, told what was passing in distant places, and, at certain moments, gave proof of marvellous science. In the lodges, Cagliostro, the Grand Copt, introduced a little girl of some ten years old, clad in white, with a blue girdle and a red ribbon crosswise. He called her *pupil*, or *dove*, placed her before a decanter filled with water, and breathed on her face. Then the child, looking through the decanter, saw wonderful sights, of which she gave a description. If the "dove" had been alone in the possession of this second sight, one might have treated it all as mere jugglery; but Cagliostro communicated this faculty to a whole crowd of people. It was *hydromancy*, renewed from the Gnostics and Manichæans, who themselves had it from the Devil-worshippers of still earlier times. Cagliostro was implicated in the famous "necklace" trial. He found means to have himself acquitted, but having had the audacity to return to Rome in 1783, he was there arrested, and condemned to perpetual .imprisonment, in which he died, miserably. But he had made over a million of adepts, amongst whom were found honest people and even Catholics, who took Animal Magnetism seriously, and continued its practices, without knowing them essentially.

Attentive and judicious observers, seeing Animal Magnetism produce phenomena superior to the physical and mental strength of the persons magnetized, suspected diabolical agency. They were

laughed at, and people went on, either
denying troublesome facts, or setting
forth laws of nature yet unknown. But
behold, for full a quarter of a century,
Magnetism is outdone by a new order of
facts, wherein the agency of intelligent
forces, that is to say, spirits, becomes
more and more evident. In 1846, raps
were heard by night in the chamber
of two young American women, the
Misses Fox, of Rochester, New York.
By means of signs agreed upon, they put
themselves in communication with the
rapping spirit. In the twinkling of an
eye, public attention is arrested; in
every city of the Union, people practice
spiritual telegraphy with invisible beings
who willingly enter into it. Soon, Spiritualism crosses the ocean and lands in
Europe. Like its forerunner, Magnetism, it modestly begins with phenomena simple enough, which do not immediately oblige people to acknowledge a
superhuman power. Under the pressure

of the fingers, tables move. Not much
of a prodigy this! The least lesson in
physics presents sights very exclusively
natural and much more surprising. But
wait a while. Public curiosity once excited, the enchanted furniture displays
more knowledge; it gives those who
question it very precise answers; table
feet, daily more agile, move pencils that
make drawings, write whole pages, reveal
the greatest secrets,* and, finally, preach
philosophy and religion. Thousands of

* Here is one fact, amongst a hundred others, the
authenticity of which we can certify : At a sitting of
spiritists, a pencil writes a letter to a person unknown
to those present, but whose address it gives. Next
day, one of the spiritists brings the letter to the
address marked. The person named was found there.
The paper was handed to him ; he turns pale ; the
writing was unmistakably that of his father, some
time dead. But when he had finished reading it, he
was in a frightful state. The letter contained a
severe reproach for the little care he had taken to
keep the promise made to his dying father, when
none but they themselves were present, to pay a debt
contracted by the latter !

persons are witness to these facts, a great number are duped; the whole world is stirred; the devils enter into habitual communication with the impious or the imprudent, by whom they are invoked; a new and fearful evolution of magic begins.

Attention! Hitherto all that spirit magic shows us appears futile; but it is a beginning. Curious experiences are succeeded by preachings. Confidence once gained, the spirits can lead their credulous hearers far, very far. "To galvanic vibrations (wrote M. de Mirville in 1854, in reference to America) sermons have succeeded, then doctrines, then all the mystical societies, then clubs by hundreds, then a frantic socialism, then a vigorous attack on all religious laws; and although there is, amongst us, as yet only question of walking tables and hats, who knows but, in a few years, we shall contemplate the wrecks of their passage?"

XV.

SOME VERY WORTHY MEN BELIEVE IN THE AGENCY OF GOOD SPIRITS ; ARE THEY IN ERROR?

Most certainly they are. Let us first speak of good spirits. What leads to the belief in their agency, are disclosures of a religious character, moral advice, exhortations to do well, proceeding from invisible speakers. People do not pause to remark that the conduct of these spirits is precisely the habitual conduct of heretics and revolutionaries. To insinuate themselves into the minds of honest people, disturbers loudly give out great principles of morality, of honor, of charity; they cunningly represent the men or the institutions they seek to overthrow as hostile to these principles, and thus produce FANATICISM, which is nothing else than *generosity of sentiment placed at the service of an error.*

If the evil spirits preached *only truth and virtue*, they would be doing our business and not their own; if they preached *only error and vice*, they would horrify any one not totally depraved and corrupt. Their skill consists in wrapping up the poison in the sugar-plum. Yes, the modern spirits in case of need extol the Gospel, like Jean Jacques; justice, like Proudhon; purity of heart, like George Sand; and even Catholicism, like M. Renan. Thereupon, honest souls, too loyal to believe in perfidy, and, on the other hand, sufficiently well satisfied, *unknown to themselves*, to meet a religion entirely new, much less frightful in its threats and much more accommodating in its morality than old Catholicity, give those spirits a confidence which may lead to the abyss. We, therefore, beseech these honest and upright souls to meditate well on the following observations:

1. In the most remote times, the devils

made use of practices just the same as those we now witness, to accredit the most monstrous errors, and the most infamous practices. Those oracles of Paganism who demanded, now human sacrifices, now the most frightful outrages on modesty, had for organs objects which moved of themselves, "tables," says Tertullian, "letters which mysteriously formed themselves into lines, noises, and intelligible answers going forth from wood and stone." Even now, the idolaters of the barbarian world communicate in this way with the wicked spirits who help them in their senseless and cruel customs. The African of Dahomey consults his calabash as the Paris spiritist consults his table, and he receives abominable orders, which he executes with a terrible docility.

2. The good angels, also, have placed themselves in communication with man, but in other conditions. It was usually under the human form, sometimes under

a symbolical form; amongst the Jews, by a special favor, they answered in the name of God, when interrogated by the priest in the holy place; but never did those princes of the heavenly court place themselves in dependence on man, to come, at a call, and prattle, like gossips, with Peter and Paul, or whoever takes a notion to satisfy his curiosity. Above all, never were they seen to mingle with the demons, to converse in the same places and by the same "mediums" with all comers.

3. These pretended revealers of a more perfect religion have no understanding amongst themselves. The twelve Apostles, who founded the Catholic Church, and their countless successors, proclaimed everywhere the same creed, and so the testimony of one is strengthened and confirmed by the testimony of all the others. When a priest to-day teaches Catholic truth, two hundred and fifty-nine popes, ninety thousand bishops, millions

of priests, doctors, martyrs, saints, the learned, myriads of the faithful, the noblest portion of mankind, the most enlightened and virtuous for over eighteen hundred years, in one magnificent concert, teach with him. The distinctive sign of truth shines forth, *Unity!* But, behold, in one parlor, a table writes this, whilst in another chamber, not many yards distant, another table writes that. Is it that ignorant or lying spirits meet? How is sincerity to be distinguished from imposture, in their language? A table has told the truth to-day; who knows if it will not lie to-morrow?

Protestantism has been irrevocably condemned before Reason by the unstableness and incoherency of its doctrines. Bossuet crushed it by the irrefutable argument: "You vary; therefore you are not the truth." Spiritism is no less fruitful in whims and changes: *it varies; therefore it is not the truth.*

4. Where the revelations of spiritism

are least discordant, there is always to
be found the open or ill-disguised nega-
tion of the revelation given by the King
of spirits, assisted by the spirits of light,
amidst prodigies before which the paltry
tricks of our contemporary magic fade
into nothing. Blind brethren, open,
then, your eyes! Your spirits move
some pieces of furniture; the Divine
Revealer commanded the sea, and at
His word its waves grew calm. Your
spirits make phantoms appear; the Divine Revealer raised the dead. Your
spirits say they are able to cure some
sick persons, without furnishing any very
authentic proofs thereof; the Divine
Revealer instantly healed crowds of the
sick who were brought to Him from all
parts. Your spirits make short-dated
predictions, and are confounded by the
event; the Divine Revealer foretold
events the most distant and the most
unlikely, and all were accomplished.
The Divine Revealer never deceived, nor

was deceived; your spirits every day—yourselves admit—are caught in the fact either of ignorance or falsehood.

That a man, carried away by the impetuosity of passion, preoccupied with business, wholly given up to the ambition of advancing, or the desire of enriching himself, having usually, moreover, but very inadequate religious instruction, loses sight of evangelical truth, may be conceived. But to abandon Christian revelation, so well proved, that, in despite of the sacrifices it requires and the furious attacks it has undergone, it subsists and reigns still; to attach one's self to the suspicious and confused revelations of spirits whose identity and sincerity it is impossible to establish,* is to offer the most violent outrage to reason.

* These spirits have their apostles of flesh and blood, apostles who are also fond of shrouding themselves in mystery. The most active would seem to be *Allan Kardec;* but what! that name of Allan

5. The attitude of the revealing spirits
lacks the dignity which becomes good
angels. As in the times of Paganism,
their prodigies are juggler's tricks, incomplete prodigies, wherein weakness
betrays itself side by side with strength,
silly prodigies, more apt to gratify the
vanity of those who perform, and the
curiosity of those who see them, than to
glorify God and sanctify souls; prodigies
which leave after them an impression,
not of peace, but of trouble and dis-
quietude. Their language is still more
pitiful than their acts. Useless words,
hazy but emphatic verbiage, often sufficiently INDECENT, sudden transitions,
which follow up edifying counsels by
others of a very different kind. No,
good spirits speak not thus.

Kardec hides another, which profane I do not know.
Another sells at a high price books which he signs
Eliphas Lévi. He is supposed to be a certain Levite,
who, having cast his soutane to the winds, became a
magician, for want of something better. Such are
the apostles, the great initiators of spiritism.

The language of the angels of light, like that of the Word made flesh, may be simple and popular, but it is always dignified.

6. The tree is known by its fruits. What are the fruits of spiritism?

In the physical order: no serious and useful progress; vain illusions, and, at the utmost, the equivocal and temporary relief of some infirmities; on the other hand, all nervous diseases, and others which spring from an over-excited imagination, and which, as we are about to show, end frequently in madness.

In the intellectual order: a prop given to five or six errors, which, from age to age, rise up against Catholic dogmas; a pale repetition, under an apocalyptic form, of sophisms which have grown stale in anti-religious journals. The spirits of falsehood say themselves what they made human voices say; that is all.

In the moral order: disasters, madness, suicide. In many a place, revelations

more or less in accordance with truth
sow dissensions in families. *Insane asylums are filled with spiritists*, whom the
spirits have put out of their mind.

From 1820 to 1870, the number of
lunatics has increased threefold. Of
two hundred and fifty-five mad people in
one asylum, fifty-four were victims of
spiritism !

A disgust for life takes possession of
the unfortunates who hold intercourse
with him who was " a murderer from the
beginning." At Tours, two old men
made away with themselves ; at Lyons,
a woman cut herself in both arms with a
razor, inflicting incurable wounds. These
sad occurrences are multiplied from day
to day. Let those who have eyes to see,
open them, before their bewitchment is
complete and irremediable.

The relations between the good angels
and man produce no such doubts ; they
increase his faith, his courage, and his
peace.

XVI.

SPIRITISM AND THE CALLING UP OF THE DEAD.

When the spirits who put tables and such like objects in motion are asked to indicate their name and quality, they very frequently declare themselves to be the soul of such and such a dead person, and if invoked under that name, they willingly answer. On this account it is that a numerous class of spiritualists deny the existence of pure spirits, good or bad, and replace them by the souls of the departed.

We are far from denying the possibility of apparitions of the dead. The history, even of Catholicity, presents examples enough of such apparitions. St. Peter appears to Attila, and frightens him; St. Aloysius Gonzagua appears to St. Catherine in the splendor of celestial glory; the Blessed Germaine appears to the Lady of Beauregard, and cures her; St. Perpetua sees her brother, Dinocratius, in the torments of purgatory, etc. Holy Scripture itself relates the apparition of Samuel to Saul, that of Onias and Jeremiah to Judas Maccabeus, that of the Crucified to Paul, on the road to Damascus.

Evocation is not even condemned if it be inspired by God, and effected in His name. The Roman Breviary relates a memorable example thereof, on the day of the 7th of May, feast of St. Stanislaus, bishop.

Poland had for her king Boleslaus, whom the saint, a new John the Baptist, had deeply offended, by publicly reproving his notorious misconduct. The prince, in a solemn assembly of the kingdom, cited the bishop before him, as the wrongful possessor of a small farm, bought in the name of his Church. The title deeds were wanting; the witnesses did not dare to speak. Stanislaus prom-

ises that, in three days, he will bring
Peter, the or ginal owner of the farm,
who was dead three years. The promise
is greeted with laughter (as it would be
now;) but the man of God, after three
days of fasting and prayer, orders Peter
to rise from his sepulchre. The latter
comes to life again, follows the bishop to
court, and before the king and his terror-
stricken courtiers, declares that he really
sold his field to the bishop, and was
by him paid the price thereof; he then
slept again in the Lord.

Relations between this world and the
world beyond the tomb are not impossible; but the illusion of the spiritists
consists in persuading themselves that by
means of certain formula the barrier
which has hitherto separated them can
be broken down. This error dates from
the highest antiquity. It is noticed by
St. Augustine in these terms: "Those
spirits are deceivers, not by nature, but
by malice. They make themselves gods

and *souls of the departed*, but they do not make themselves devils, for they really are so." (*City of God*, X, II.)

A learned physician of the sixteenth century, John Wier, made, in his turn, the following reflections :

"Think not that it is very hard for the Devil to represent falsely the figure of disembodied spirits, and to frighten, by apparitions, the heirs of the deceased and others ; this is done in order to force the simple, and those who have little trust in God to do unlawful services, under the shadow of religion, according to the form thereof imposed upon them. He also tries to confound those who are firm in the faith, and takes every means of shaking them ; to enrich, by promises, the desperate, the credulous, the foolish, to destroy those whom he allures by the hope of a rich inheritance, and to torment them by the fear of ill fortune." (*Imposture of the Devils.*)

Undoubtedly the supposed dead bring

pretended proofs of their identity, but these proofs are no wise conclusive. They remind you of peculiarities which the dead and you alone knew; the mysterious pencil imitates his writing: all that may be. But the devils were invisible witnesses of those peculiarities; doubtless they can skilfully counterfeit handwriting, they who work prodigies much more extraordinary. And they know enough of the human heart to know that in persuading you a beloved one is there conversing with you, they will secure a better hearing, when, with pretended simplicity, they boldly declare that Catholic teaching is deceptive. These invisible interlocutors take the most august names, such as that of St. Louis, and even of St. Paul; and under these names they contradict the faith of St. Louis and the teachings of St. Paul, and repeat, like parrots, the humanitarian phrases of our modern philosophers. But history shows that there have been authentic apparitions of the glorious dead, attested by miracles; not one of them declared that he was mistaken when he believed and taught Catholic dogmas during his mortal life. What matters it, then, that these late comers, who, taking at random the names of our Saints and those of the heroes of free thought, emphatically proclaim some errors resuscitated before them by a dozen scribblers notoriously unbelieving?

To conjure up the pretended souls of the departed is an old Pagan practice that was punished with death in the legislation dictated by God to Moses. Had it been the will of Providence to authorize this intercourse with the world beyond the grave, it would have, assuredly, determined the conditions thereof, mankind would have known them, and not have been reduced to these suspicious and unwarranted manœuvres, which can only give our souls doubt, trouble, and the most terrible agitation.

XVII.

SOME GOOD CHRISTIANS THINK THEY CAN
MAKE TABLES SPEAK, THE CHURCH NOT
HAVING YET DECIDED THEREON.

Christians who are ignorant or pre-
sumptuous even to obstinacy, yes; excellent Christians, assuredly not.

There are now-a-days Christians of
many kinds: sincere Catholics who deny
what the Church affirms, respectful Catholics who ridicule what the Church hon-
ors, submissive Catholics who do what
the Church forbids, and not what she
commands. We have met with a distinguished mathematician who declared himself more a Catholic than ourselves, yet
did not even believe in the personal existence of God!

Undoubtedly, men who are reputed
good Catholics communicate needlessly
with the spirits. But are not men seen
to fall into faults of pride, of avarice, of

sensuality, of hatred, of sloth, deceiving
the priest who admits them to the sacra-
ments, or deceiving themselves? Great
God! if we permit ourselves all that
such or such a one, who is not avowedly
irreligious, permits himself, whither shall
we go?

The Church, which has formally condemned all voluntary communications
with the devils, has not as yet pronounced,
we acknowledge, *on the form which magic
assumes now-a-days*, one of those solemn
decisions, which, after long and patient
researches on the nature of observed
facts, at length publicly condemns them;
but the Church has not remained silent.
A great number of bishops have spoken.
In France, in Canada, and other countries, eminent prelates have prohibited
all communication with spirits or spiritualists. Priests renowned for their learning and their eloquence, such as Padre
Ventura, Père de Ravignan, Père Lacor-
diare, energetically opposed this new

form of sorcery. It would be difficult for us to give an exact list of the prelates who have condemned spiritism. . . . But where, in a religious question, immediately practical, *no pontiff has approved, many formally condemned*, the Christian who dares to meddle with it is guilty of the most evident temerity.

Furthermore, Rome has not ignored these strange manifestations; she quickly perceived their dangerous character; the Eternal City knows perfectly well that Pius IX, without having as yet fulminated a public anathema, strongly condemns the practices of spiritism, and encourages the bishops who condemn, and the writers who oppose it.

In the fifth century, St. Augustine, one of the greatest geniuses the world has ever seen, wrote, in the immortal book of the "Confessions:" "Many people, desirous of returning to Thee, O Lord, and being unable of themselves, have recourse to pure spirits, and, falling into

the desire of curious visions, deserved to
become the sport of illusions. Bèing
proud, they sought Thee; swelling out,
rather than striking their breast, and
then they found, in the ways of pride,
those Powers of the air who were to deceive them by the employment of their
magic power. The Devil transformed
himself into an angel of light. That
false mediator, whom the secret judg-
ments of God permits to seduce the
proud, has sin in common with man; not
being clothed in a mortal body, he would
fain appear eternal, like God; but the
true Mediator, whom the humble know
well how to recognize, is Jesus Christ,
mortal with men, just with God." (X,
42, 43.)

Jesus Christ, the true Mediator, the
Divine Revealer, founded the Church, to
which He said: "He that heareth you,
heareth me." Now, whoever hears the
Church cannot hear the revelations of
spiritism. Either Catholic, with sixty

generations of saints, or spiritist, with
some enthusiasts of yesterday, those con-
cerned have to choose. The two doctrines are, moreover, on the gravest
points, in evident contradiction; if spiritism were right, the Church would have
to disappear, and the fate of mankind
would remain at the mercy of a troop
of those invisible and unknown goblins
whose language is more confused than
that of Babel! Marvellous progress!

XVIII.

IS IT, THEN, A GREAT FAULT TO CONVERSE
   WITH THE SPIRITS, PROVIDED ONE DOES
   NOT GIVE UP THEIR FAITH?

Most certainly.

The conversation of the wicked, be
they who they may, is full of danger.
Necessity or charity alone excuse it.
"Tell me what company you frequent,
and I will tell you who you are." You
are the father of a family; your child is

good, candid, amiable, virtuous. Some
one proposes to you to introduce him
amongst young people, who are well instructed and very clever, fit to make their
way and help him in after days to make
his, but spoiled to the marrow of their
bones; will you throw him into the society of such companions? The more
graceful their manners are, the more
agreeable their conversation, the more
amiable they appear, the more they are
to be feared. Truly, the assurance of
men now-a-days is something astound-
ing! One would think they were all
inaccessible to seduction, to error; they
seem to have received a diploma of moral
and intellectual infallibility! What! you
imagine that you can converse unscathed
with that old deceiver, who has on his
side, together with the enormous superiority of his intelligence, and sixty centuries of reflection and experience, the
bewilderment you will naturally feel in
entering, alone, upon an unknown world

to which he will guide you! He who un-
necessarily opens a bad book deserves to
be blinded by it. What would be the
blindness of him who, in spite of the
warnings which God gives him by His
Church, would converse with the spirit
who dictates or inspires all bad books?

Be candid. What do you wish to learn
of these spirits? Things that God con-
ceals from you, the secrets of the unseen
world, or of the future. You ask of your
tables and your pencils all that superstition asked of magic in all ages. You
consider it a very simple thing to ask a
rebel treacherously to give up to you
your sovereign's secret. You, perchance,
even ask him for help and succor in escaping the Divine will. And do you not
fear that your sacrilegious curiosity may
be answered by falsehood? You make
the unfaithful servant chatter, because
the master is silent, or speaks in a way
that is distasteful to your self-indulgence,
and you think all that innocent, and free

from danger! It is only fun, you say! Very good; but do you suppose that the proud enemy of mankind, whose envy has been the cause of all our woes, would lend himself to your whims, like an obedient dog, if he expected to gain nothing by his complacency? Listening to him, you gradually become his disciple; he chooses, indeed, to be your slave for a time, because from slave he will insensibly make himself master.

These experiments are very amusing, you will say. I answer you, with St. Peter Chrysologus: "He who pretends to amuse himself with the Devil shall not rejoice with Christ." All that amuses is not allowable. Certain romances are very interesting, very piquant, very diverting; and yet, if you read them, you will kill your soul.

Let the priest, in the exercise of his Divine functions, let particular men, with the charitable end of opening the eyes of their blinded brethren, interrogate the devils and answer them ; they have grave reasons for so doing, and they may count on the protection of Providence. But they know how unhealthy is the diabolical atmosphere, and the two men, as learned as they are devoted, to whom we are indebted for the most learned researches on these subjects, Mr. de Mirville and Mr. G. Desmousseaux, no longer assist at these diabolical operations, because, being sufficiently informed, they rightly consider that *mere curiosity does not justify the presence of a Christian at those meetings.*

St. Paul, writing to the early faithful, forbade them to eat the meats sacrificed to idols, because those meats had been consecrated to the devils. "You cannot be partakers of the table of the Lord and of the table of the devils." (I Cor., x, 21:) To converse with the devils is a far graver thing than to eat meats which were offered to them. To those who imprudently question them apply, therefore, the saying of the Apostle : "I would not that you should be made partakers with devils. Do we provoke the Lord to jealousy ? Are we stronger than He?" (1 Cor., x, 20, 22.)

XIX.

WHAT DIFFERENCE IS THERE BETWEEN MAGNETIC CLAIRVOYANCE AND SPIRITISM?

None, at bottom; only, in magnetism, the Devil first hid his object under cover of certain phenomena which might be produced by causes purely physical. There have been, and still are, men who practice magnetism in good faith. They are, without knowing it, the co-operators of the arch enemy. The Devil serves them gratis, because that is his own affair, and attracts an audience whom he will turn to account. Innocent children become, as in spiritism, his instruments, just as they sometimes are the instruments of wicked men whose evil designs they unwittingly execute. The most famous magnetizers now acknowledge the superhuman agency of the spirits in magnetic prodigies.

Let us hear Baron du Potet relate how it came to pass that, while wanting only to be a magnetizer, he became a magician :

"Does not history preserve for us the sad example of what befel past generations in regard to sorcery? The facts were but too real. . . . But how did I find that art? By producing, under my eyes, at first without my seeking them, undoubted facts of sorcery. . . .

"And, in fact, what is the magnetic sleep? A result of magic power. And what determines those attractions, those sudden inclinations, those fits of fury, those dislikes, those crises, those convulsions, which may be rendered permanent, if it be not the very principle employed, the agency most certainly known by the men of the past? That which you call *nervous*, or *magnetic fluid*, the ancients called *occult power*. . . .

"I have felt the attacks of that terrible power; one day, that evoked force, *another would say* (and say well) THAT DEMON, agitated my whole being. . . . The bond was made, the compact was concluded, an occult power was mingled with the force proper to myself. . . ."

The celebrated Regazzoni delivered, by his passes, an officer who, magnetized by vengeance and from afar, (that is to say, the victim of diabolical possession,) was suffering cruelly. M. Desmousseaux asked him how he managed to do it. "I discharge the magnetic fluid." "I know; but after that?" "After that, I invoke benign spirits, in order to drive away the evil spirits." These prodigies, in fact, always produced by some magical sign, at least originally; habitually accepted, at least once, by the person magnetized, suppose the intervention of ANOTHER, as often as there is, as in second sight, not only augmentation of the power of our organs, but effect obtained without the agency of the cause which should, naturally, produce it. Under the influence of certain nervous excitements, our organs become more acute, and the ear, for instance, perceives imperceptible sounds; but the eye sees not through an opaque body. If the magnetised person sees not only through a wall, but through a number of interposing bodies, objects placed at a distance, it is that ANOTHER *shows* him what he sees. In like manner, if the magnetised person tells that which he did not know, that which he had not learned, that which he himself shall not know after the magnetic *coma*, it is that ANOTHER, who does know, comes, during the *coma*, to speak by his mouth.

Magnetism, like spiritism, boasted of being the benefactor of humanity; it is only its plague. If it has cured, or appeared to cure some diseases, it has, on the other hand, disturbed, seduced, led

astray multitudes of unhappy people; it
has, by the despotic power it gives the
magnetiser over his voluntary victim, even
out of the *coma*, produced monstrous
moral disorders. In fine, as testified by
the princes of that black art, it also gives
a disgust of life, and has even led, more
than once, to suicide.

Let us hear the grave warnings of the
Encyclical, published on the 4th of August, 1858, by Cardinal Macchi, by order
of Pius IX : "The perversity of men has
come to that degree, that, neglecting the
lawful study of science, to give themselves up to mere curiosity, to the great
ruin of souls and the great detriment of
civil society itself, they glory in having
discovered a new principle of magic and
of divination, [*hariolandi divinandique
principium.*] Thus, then, thanks to the
influence of mesmerism and of *clairvoy-
ance*, as they say, silly women, excited by
'passes' which are not always conformable to the laws of decency, make them-

selves strong to see the invisible, to discourse on religion itself, to conjure up the souls of the dead, to receive answers, to find out things hidden and distant; they have the rash audacity to practise these and other acts of superstition, bringing thus a considerable profit to themselves and their masters.* In all that, whatever be their art or their imposture, as physical means are found applied to bring about effects which are not natural; there is a deception wholly unlawful and tinctured with heresy, and at the same time a scandal against propriety and good morals."

Magnetism, like spiritism, usually becomes fatal, even in this world, to those who practise it. About the year 1843, China witnessed a recrudescence of the *old custom* of corresponding with spirits, nearly as it is done in Europe at the

---

* Clearly alluding to that young girl possessed of a divining spirit, who was exorcised by the Apostle St. Paul.

present day; but that did not last long, because Chinese good sense remarked that "*much evil came of it*, and never the least good." (*Overland China Mail*, quoted by M. Desmousseaux.)

A warning to some Catholics who still think that mesmerism is harmless and even beneficial; a warning, too, to those who consult *clairvoyantes* or mesmerisers.

XX.

IS THE DEVIL THE HEAD OF SECRET SOCIETIES?

Scathing question! For many ages there have been underground associations whose members, clandestinely combined, bound by oaths, submissive to an occult direction, have been on various occasions, excommunicated by the Sovereign Pontiffs. (Constitutions of Clement XII, Benedict XIV, Pius VII.) It is entirely useless to demonstrate the Satanic nature of these societies to those who are ever so little acquainted with them; but it is very necessary to open the eyes of honest people who have become their dupes, or are in danger of becoming so.

"Our final end," wrote one of the high dignitaries of that gloomy empire, in 1819, "our final end is that of Voltaire and the French Revolution, the annihilation of Catholicity, and even of the Christian idea, for ever." This, then, is their object. Another will give a sketch of the proceedings: "It is decided in our councils that we want no more Christians. Let us make no martyrs, but make vice popular amongst the masses. Let them breathe it through the five senses. Make hearts vicious, and you will have no more Catholics!" If that be not diabolical language, what is?

Satan and his imps have a plan, the existence of which it is not hard to discover, nor its development to follow: *to break up the society of which the Man-God* *is the Head, and to substitute for it a society governed by the prince of darkness.**

---

* We again borrow some significant details from authentic documents published by Crétineau-Joly :

"When you have insinuated into some souls a disgust for the family and for religion—one goes almost always in the train of the other—let fall certain words that may incite the wish of being affiliated to the nearest Masonic lodge. . . . To become member of a lodge, to feel one's self called to keep a secret *never confided to you*, is for certain natures a luxury and an ambition. . . . The lodges are a sort of depot which must be passed through in order to reach us ; . . . they form, unknown to the members, our preparatory novitiate. . . . Never throw off the mask ; prowl especially round the Catholic fold. . . . In my opinion, our young neophytes are too apt to make their *religious hatred* a political hatred. The conspiracy against the Roman See ought not to be confounded with other projects. *Let us conspire only against Rome.* . . . In Paris, they will not understand that ; but in London I have seen men who get hold of our plan better." (The Church and the Revolution.)

Thus you see the *gates of hell* are trying to *prevail* against the City of God. Here are other words no less clear : "The great majority of the order not only do not admit Christianity, but opposes it with all its might." (*Masonic Review*, January, 1848.) "Christi-

This mystery of iniquity is partially accomplished; the Catholic Church is not crumbling away, and will not crumble away; but the infernal church is being formed and disciplined. It has hatred for its bond. It gives the first posts to those who most hate Jesus Christ and His mystical body; it swells its ranks from the indifferent themselves, because he who is not for Jesus Christ is against Him. Men who would neither kill, nor rob, alas! men who go to Mass, and who, in spite of the repeated *anathema* of the Holy See, approach the Holy Table, will declare to us upon their honor that they belong to a secret society, Freemasonry, for instance, and that there all religious opinions are respected, not excepting their own. Capital! the Devil is an ex-

anity is a horrible magic, the height of error, a murder." (Memoir of the Masonic Jubilee of 1833.) And yet people are astonished when the Church declares that one cannot be a Freemason and a Christian at the same time!

perienced diplomatist. He asks of each
only what he can get. He will not way-
lay the first comer at the street corner
with a dagger or a murderous shell; he
will not set a hot-headed, but honest
writer, to wage a daily war of calumny
on the Church. Each one has his own
degree of degradation or imprudence.
This one shall be an assassin; that other
a calumniator; a third, an honest man
duped, will serve, by clubbing with others, to hire the assassin and the calumniator, and, by his reputation for probity,
give the association an appearance of
honesty. But, in fine, every secret society (the secret agreement of an oppressed
people to drive out an oppressive conqueror is not a secret society) is stamped
with the seal of Satan.

1. *The oath taken therein is Satanic.*
Man may, and should, obey the orders of
superiors who, in families, in the State,
in the Church, are the depositaries of
God's authority; he has no right to divest

himself of his liberty in favor of a mere human power, to become the perpetual slave of unknown chiefs who may require of him indefinite acts, perhaps even directly criminal, and consign him to the dagger if he refuse. That oath is radically null, for man cannot validly bind himself to what is immoral. But it is always a great crime to sign that compact of slavery, incorporating the signer with the gloomy cohorts whose chief is the first rebel.

2. *Affiliation to those secret societies is an evident revolt against regular social order;* the members of that underground empire uniting together only to substitute here below, by stratagem or by violence, for providential order that devised by their chief.

3. *The right of life and death adjudged in those societies* (and from time to time exercised) *is a usurpation of the right of God,* communicated only to His lieutenants, that is to say, the visible conductors of nations; hence, it follows that those

who accept that savage right, do thereby virtually become assassins.

Unknown brethren, who read these pages, in the name of your dignity as Christians and as men, fly these secret societies. The most peaceable of them, Freemasonry, has, even in our own day, driven from Portugal the daughters of Charity; formed, in Belgium, associations for the extirpation of Christian habits; and, in France, testified in a striking manner its hatred for the temporal sovereignty of the Holy See, now the essential condition of the independence of the Church;* what must be thought of the others? Some writers state that, in the inner circles of some, Satan has been, and still is, directly and personally adored.† It is very natural that the occult sciences

---

* Since the above was written the temporal power has fallen beneath the persistent attacks of the secret societies. For how long, God only knows. (TRANS.)

† The learned author of the "Jew of Verona," Bresciani, states that he had certain proof of it.

should be practiced in the darkness of occult societies; what is certain, from all that has transpired of their machinations, and the solemn decisions of the

Here is what the lamented Charles Sainte-Foi substantially relates, (Translation of Goerres' "Mystical," epilogue :)

"Happening to be in one of the most important capitals of Europe, a clergyman, a friend of ours, made the acquaintance of a gentleman well versed in chemistry and other natural sciences, little disposed, consequently, to prejudice or spiritual delusion, having, moreover, lived far from religion, and was converted only a little before. This gentleman had heard people speak of secret societies, in which revolutionary doctrines were combined with the practice of necromancy. (As in the Egyptian Freemasonry of Cagliostro. . . .) Impelled by curiosity, he got himself admitted into one of these associations, each of which was, I believe, composed of twelve members, and whose meetings took place by night. He there witnessed some very extraordinary things. *The initiated entered, by means of magnetic somnambulism, into connection with the dead, who appeared to them and answered their questions.* On his return home, he wished to make himself sure that there had been no illusion or deceit, and tried to obtain the same results, by magnetising his son, about eleven or twelve years old. Having

Church, is, that they are the instruments of the infernal powers in their struggle against Christ and His faithful people; that they are the *synagogue of Satan*, the earthly army of anti-Christianity, hateful, hypocritical, murderous. The secret societies are the central focus of revolution, and " REVOLUTION (said Pius IX, in his Encyclical of December 8, 1853) IS INSPIRED BY SATAN HIMSELF. *Its object is to destroy from top to bottom the edifice of Christianity*, and to reconstruct on its ruins, *the social order of Paganism*." Paganism, is the public reign of the evil spirits substituted for that of God.

put him to sleep, he conjured up the shade of his wife, whom he had lost when that son was not quite two years old. The child, in his sleep, depicted his mother, and with a pencil drew on paper a very good portrait of her features and her dress. The priest, having consented to be magnetised, sees, in his turn, the wife of the magnetiser and several other dead persons. But on awaking, he felt himself in some way the slave of a foreign power, and feared a real possession. The gentleman, frightened at what had happened, set out for Rome."

XXI.

WHAT IS DIABOLICAL TEMPTATION?

It is the effort made by the wicked
spirits to incite each one of us to do evil.
The word temptation signifies proof.   To
merit reward we must encounter trials.
Two sorts of trials await us here below:
first, *temptation purely human*, such as the
sight of beautiful fruit, which one is for-
bidden to eat; secondly, *diabolical temptation*, which often brings on, usually in-
creases, the other.

The Devil attacks men in three ways:
by suggestion, by snare, and by possession.

Suggestion is the most usual form of
diabolical temptation.   An invisible enemy comes upon us, he sows in our imagination bad thoughts, he keeps them up,
brings them back, in spite of our efforts
to drive them away; he excites and stirs
up our senses themselves; we feel our-

selves interiorly harassed, incited, drawn away; it is like a discourse without words, but urgent and violent. It even happens that these detestable thoughts beset and pursue with still greater fury those who devote themselves to practices of piety; pious persons often hear, even at the moment of death, and against their will, these troublesome thoughts. The most dangerous suggestions are those which adapt themselves to our tastes, foster our inclinations, excuse our cowardice, inflame our self-love, and turn us away, noiselessly and insensibly, from the right road.

To the suggestion is joined the snare. External objects, and, above all, persons under his influence, the Devil makes use of as instruments to bring together a concurrence of circumstances which suddenly seize upon the unwary Christian, and cast him into the abyss. An obstinate hunter, Satan knows how to foresee and await. We can understand, from the

history of Weishaupt, the modern reno-
vator of secret societies, and the terrible
craft of the means which that wretch
recommends for corrupting men *insensibly*, what must be the skill of the master
of whom Weishaupt was but a mere disciple. Nothing is more degrading than
to make one's self the servant of that
murderer of souls, by helping him to lay
his snares for them. Yet this is what is
done by the authors of bad books, those
who spread them, and those who lend
them; this is what is done by all those
who voluntarily scandalize their neighbor.

Possession belongs to a class of extraordinary facts which only happen by
the special permission of God. Then
the Devil, even without being called,
shows himself under frightful forms; he
causes strange noises to be heard; in a
word, he tempts EXTERIORLY.

Who does not know the history of St.
Anthony, related by St. Athanasius, one
of the greatest geniuses that ever shed

glory on mankind? When scarcely twenty years of age, Anthony, filled with a desire for perfection, had distributed his fortune to the poor, and retired to the desert to practice perfection. The demon there harassed him in every way. First, he incites in the mind of the young solitary thoughts of regret, then the most wearisome anxiety; finally, violent incitements to lust.

Overcome by prayer and mortification, the Devil has recourse to means the most extraordinary; first, frightful voices, then apparitions under the form of a shameless woman. Being always repulsed, the infernal spirit tries to inspire his conqueror with feelings of pride. He presents himself under the form of a black dwarf, and tells him: "I have deceived many people, and have overthrown many great personages, but I confess myself vanquished by thee."

After a while, the struggle began anew, fierce and terrible. Horrible forms of lions, bears, and serpents appeared with frightful noises; the Saint was violently struck; but, all covered with bruises as he was, he invoked Our Lord Jesus Christ, and added a new triumph to those he had already gained.

Although very rare in ordinary life, obsession is very frequent in the heroic life of the Saints. During a great part of his beautiful life, the Curé of Ars knew that trial. "Usually," says his biographers, "at midnight, three great blows on the outer door warned the Curé of Ars of the presence of his enemy. After having amused himself by raising a horrible clatter on the staircase, the Devil entered. . . . He betook himself to the bed-curtains, clutched them and shook them furiously. Often he cried out in a scoffing tone: 'Vianey, Vianey, *eater of truffles*, we shall have thee!' . . . or else he drove nails into the floor. One day, the good Curé compared the tumultuous noise of the fiends to that of an army of

Austrians, or said that the devils had held their parliament in his yard."

These fierce attacks of the Devil were a hard cross for the holy priest; he consoled himself with the remark that each victory over the fiend was followed by a signal favor, or the conversion of some noted sinner.

Persons of a nervous temperament and lively imagination imagine themselves haunted by the Devil, when there is nothing of the kind. People should not believe in obsession without the most convincing proof.

XXII.

WHAT IS DIABOLICAL POSSESSION?

It is a rough imitation, a sort of infernal parody on the incarnation of the Word, permitted by Providence, in order to show what would one day become of man if he preferred the service of the

Prince of Darkness to that of the King of Heaven.

A possessed person is one whose body, and even, indirectly, his spiritual faculties (except the will, which never belongs to Satan, unless with its own consent) are given up for a time to one or more devils who make him their instrument.

Possession was a known fact, and even of frequent occurrence prior to the coming of Our Lord Jesus Christ, who, during the three years of His public life, delivered a multitude of the possessed. "He went about," says the Apostle Peter, "doing good and healing all that were oppressed by the Devil." (Acts, x, 38.) The Chananeau fell at his feet, saying: "Have mercy on me, O Lord, for my daughter is grievously troubled by a devil." Jesus commands, and the fiend departs. (St. Matth., xv, 22.) St. Luke relates, in the eighth chapter of his gospel, a terrible and instructive instance of possession. "Jesus met," says he, "a certain man who had a devil now for a long time, and he wore no clothes, neither did he abide in a house, but in the tombs. And when he saw Jesus, he fell down before him, and crying out with a loud voice, he said: 'What have I to do with Thee, Jesus, Son of the Most High God? I beseech Thee, do not torment me.'" It is not the unhappy man who is possessed that speaks thus; it is the Devil who speaks by his mouth. "For," continues St. Luke, "He commanded the unclean spirit to go out of the man. For many times it seized him; and he was bound with chains, and kept in fetters; and he broke the bonds," by diabolical power, "and was driven by the devil into the deserts. And Jesus asked him, saying: 'What is thy name?' But he said: 'Legion,' because many devils were entered into him." Jesus having permitted these devils to enter into a herd of swine, caused the herd to precipitate itself into the sea. Even so would they fain drive the herd of the wicked into the sea of eternal woe! But what becomes of this man who had so long been a furious lunatic? Delivered from the devils, restored to himself, behold him sitting peacefully, covered with his garments, at the feet of his Liberator, and offering to follow Him everywhere. Who knows exactly what part the Devil may play even now, in the strange and manifold infirmities which are known by the general name of insanity? Among those numerous victims of spiritism confined in lunatic asylums, may there not be some whom the exorcisms of the Church might cure? M. de Roys, a former pupil of the Polytechnic School, proposes this question before us; the future will, perhaps, solve it.

Possessions became gradually more rare as the kingdom of Christ extended its limits. They never entirely ceased, even in Christian countries. Every one knows the famous challenge of Tertullian

to the Pagans of his time: "Let a man
who is known to be possessed by devils,
be brought before your tribunals; let a
Christian, no matter who he be, command that spirit to speak; he will confess that he is truly a devil, and, moreover, that he falsely calls himself a God.
Let them bring likewise one of those who
believe themselves moved by a god, who,
breathing strongly on the altars, have in-
haled divinity with the air. . . . If, not
daring to lie to a Christian, they confess
not that they are demons, shed, on the
spot, the blood of that rash Christian."
(Apolog., XXIII.)   St. Paulinus, in the
Life of St. Felix of Nola, declares that
he saw a possessed man walk right up
the arch of a church, head downwards,
without his clothes being disturbed, and
this man was cured at the tomb of St.
Felix.

St. Jerome (*Epitaph. Paulæ*) relates
numerous cases of possession. "At the
tomb of St. John the Baptist, Paula was

horrified to hear the roaring of devils. 'The possessed,' she said, ' howled, barked, whistled. . . . Others turned head over heels on the ground. Women were held up in the air, head downward, and yet remained covered.'"

The illustrious doctor, in his "Life of St. Hilarion," relates that every day furious animals possessed by the demon were brought to the Saint. One day, there was brought to him an enormous camel which had killed several persons; it was dragged along by more than thirty men, with great ropes; its eyes were bloodshot, its mouth frothing, its tongue swollen and constantly moving; its frightful roaring filled the air with a strange and dismal sound. Hilarion ordered him to be unbound. Those who had brought him thither refused; one only dared to obey. Hilarion advances, and says to the demon, "Whether thou art in a fox, or a camel, thou art always the same; thou dost not frighten me." Then, holding out his hand, he stands firm, and the beast, who came as fierce as though he would have devoured him, falls immediately to the ground head foremost.

Phernel, physician to Henri II, of France, and the famous Protestant surgeon, Ambroise Paré, makes mention of a possessed person who spoke Greek and Latin without having learned either. The possession of Loudun, under Louis XIII, is authenticated by historical proof the most incontestible. More recently, an epidemic of possession broke forth in a village of the Upper Alps, named Morzine, after some spiritual sittings, and of all the remedies tried, exorcisms and pilgrimages were alone successful.

The indications whereby possession is recognized are, according to Dr. Ferraris, the following: Speaking languages not previously learned; having an instinctive horror for religious objects; throwing themselves down precipices; possessing all at once a science not acquired before; remaining so firmly fixed in the place where they are, that several persons could not move them from it; suffering from the application of blessed objects, and relics, even when not aware of their presence; answering an unspoken question, or obeying a command equally unspoken. (Magnetism producing the greater part of these effects, how can we but see that it is nothing else than temporary possession?)

When these indications, or other similar ones have, by their accumulation or repetition, proved that a man is moved by a superior, and, consequently, foreign force; when, on the other hand, there is no reason to presume that these supernatural facts, wrought in him, come from God or His angels, efforts must be made for his deliverance by making use of the means which the Church, the depository of the power of Christ, has at her disposal.

At the present time, pursuant to wise rules, the ordinary of the diocese alone decides as to whether there is cause for exorcism, and appoints the exorcist.

XXIII.

WHAT IS EXORCISM?

" Exorcism is a ceremony in which the ministers of the Church authoritatively command the devils to leave at liberty the persons of whose bodies they have taken possession, and to depart from other creatures whom those malignant spirits sometimes abuse, by God's permission, since they have been in some degree subjected to them by the loss man sustained, through his sin, of the empire he had over them." (*Roman Ritual for the use of the Diocese of Bordeaux,* inst. XI.)

The Church exorcises, with prayers particularly solemn, the oil which is to

be consecrated by the bishop on Holy
Thursday, to be employed in the ceremonies of Baptism, Confirmation, Extreme Unction, and Holy Orders; the
holy water used in particular benedic-
tions, and in conflict with the spirits of
darkness; the bodies of catechumens,
that is to say, of children or adults who,
by baptism, are about to pass from the
empire of Satan to that of Jesus Christ,
and the bodies of the possessed, that is
to say, those, into whom, even after baptism, (God ordaining it, for their punishment, or tolerating it to increase their
merit,) the devils enter, or in some sort
become incarnate.

The order of Exorcist, the second of
the minor orders, confers the radical
power to make exorcisms; but when there
is question of possession, the bishops, in
preference, appoint a priest invested with
more abundant grace. Almost always,
the evil spirits resist for some time, the
commands of the exorcist, until at last,

overcome by a superior power, they proclaim, by their flight, the victory of Jesus Christ.

As regards the formula, it is varied according to the times.

We find, in the Apostolical Constitutions, this adjuration: "O Thou who hast bound the strong arm and broken his weapons, . . . Only Son of the Father, chastise these malignant spirits, and deliver from their torments the works of Thy hands." In the Middle Ages longer prayers were voluntarily used; the Saints and Mary were invoked; sometimes, they scolded the Devil, calling him baker, or cook of hell, (*pistor, coquus Acherontis.*) The learning of some exorcists not being equal to their faith, their formulas were not free from puerility, or superstition. But the Church was not slow in rectifying them. At the present day the prudence of ecclesiastical authority is extreme, and no impropriety is to be feared.

XXIV.

DO MEANS EXIST WHEREBY THE LAITY MAY EFFECTUALLY COMBAT SATAN?

Undoubtedly: but not in their own proper strength. Before a spirit man is like a child before a giant. Divine assistance alone restores the equilibrium. Our first parents, not choosing to correspond with grace from above, gave way in the struggle; and becoming rebellious towards God, they found themselves slaves of Satan. In virtue of a law, apparently hard enough, in reality highly advantageous, since it permitted man's fall only to raise him higher—in virtue of the law of universal responsibility, with guilty Adam, the visible world, of which God constituted him master, and his posterity itself, fell under the power of the Devil, his conqueror. But, *immediately*, the Divine Word, to whose image man had been created, charged

Himself with expiating Adam's transgression, and procuring for all men the graces necessary for taking a splendid revenge on hell. By the future merits of Christ during forty ages, by His past merits since the sacrifice of Calvary, the weakest amongst Adam's children have triumphed and may still triumph over all the evil spirits combined against him.

"Be strengthened in the Lord," says St. Paul. "Put you on the armor of God, that you may be able to stand against the snares of the Devil. For our wrestling is not against flesh and blood, but against principalities and powers, against the rulers of the world of this darkness, against the spirits of wickedness in high places. . . . Taking in all things the shield of faith, wherewith you may be able to extinguish all the fiery darts of the most wicked one; . . . and take unto you the sword of the spirit, which is the Word of God; watch and pray." (Eph., VI.)

"Without me," said the Divine Master Himself, "you can do nothing." "No, nothing," adds the Apostle, "not even to pronounce His holy name aright; but *I can do all things in Him who strengtheneth me.*" (Phil., IV, 13.)

Thus, by recourse to the Man-God, any man may combat the Devil, and, even after a defeat, after innumerable defeats, break his chains; the gloomy empire of Satan will confine only his willing slaves, throughout eternity.

XXV.

ON HOLY WATER, THE SIGN OF THE CROSS, AND RELICS.

In the struggle against the Devil, Christians employ the spiritual weapons just named, and unbelievers find their conduct very amusing. "How," say they, " can that water, for instance, drive away the Devil, whom it cannot even touch,

since he has no body?" The Christian
answers: "It is not the water that puts
the Devil to flight; it is the blessing. A
blessing is a spiritual virtue, which God
gives to a material object, in order that
we may make use of it at the proper
time. The object blessed becomes thus,
by the will of God, the vehicle of a grace
conformable to the blessing it has received."

Now, behold what the blessing of the
water is:

"I exorcise thee, creature of water: in
the name of God, the Father Almighty,
in the name of Jesus Christ, His Son,
Our Lord, and in virtue of the Holy
Ghost, to the end that thou mayest become water exorcised to put to flight all
the powers of the enemy; to root out
and displant the enemy himself, with his
apostate angels, by virtue of Our Lord
Jesus Christ." . . .

Thanks to this prayer of the Church,
the holy water, religiously employed,

drives away the Devil, tormented, not by the water, but by the Divine virtue whereof that water is the receptacle. The use of holy water dates from the first ages of Christianity, since the Apostolical Constitutions, drawn up about the end of the fourth century, call it a means of putting the devils to flight. Good Christians always have holy water in their dwelling; they take some, at least in the morning, when they awake, and at night before going to sleep. As for others, they ought to know that, if people are not obliged to take holy water, they are obliged to respect that water, like all that the Church sanctifies by her benediction.

The virtue of the Sign of the Cross, in the conflict with Satan, is easily understood. To make that sign, is to remind him of the whole history of his defeat, to invoke against him the just reprisals of the Almighty Crucified. Hear Lactanctius declaring, before Paganism still erect, the power of that sign which is soon to give victory to those who follow it: "He will know how terrible to the devils is the sign of the cross, who shall see how, adjured by the name of Christ, they go forth from the bodies they possessed. For, as Jesus Christ, when he went about amongst men, put all the devils to flight by His word, and brought back to their usual sense their minds disturbed and crazed even to fury by the incursions of the evil spirits; so do His disciples drive away the devils by the name of their Master and the sign of His passion. The proof of this is easily given. When the Pagans offer sacrifices to their gods, if there be in the assembly any one whose forehead is marked with that sign, the sacrifices do not succeed, and the oracle cannot answer those who consult him." Lactanctius adds that, "On several occasions, the devils complaining of the presence of those profane persons who impeded their action, cruel persecution was thus excited against the faithful."

"We Christians," said St. Anthony, to the heathen philosophers who visited him in his solitude, "We Christians, by merely pronouncing the name of Jesus crucified, drive away those demons whom you worship as gods. Their charms and their influence lose all their power wherever the sign of the cross is formed." And, making the sign of the cross, before them, over the possessed, he delivered them.

By the frequent employment of the sign of the cross in exorcisms, the Church attests the power of that sign, and recommends it to her children.

The relics of the Saints are also a potent weapon against the devils. To the glorious dust of His friends God communicates a supernatural virtue, fruitful in wonders of every kind, but especially terrible to hell. Here, amongst a thousand others, is one very striking instance:

Cæsar Gallus, a very religious prince, having consecrated, at Daphné, a suburb of Antioch, opposite the Temple of Apollo, a church to the true God, under the invocation of St. Babylas, placed therein the relics of that holy martyr. Immediately the Devil was struck dumb in his temple. A little later, Julian, the Apostate, came to Antioch to restore with great pomp the worship of Apollo, and, offering to that false god victims by hundreds, besought him to continue his oracles, or at least to tell the cause of his silence. "The town of Daphné," answers the demon, "is full of *dead bodies;* let them be taken away, and I will speak." Understanding the hint, as St. Chrysostom remarks, the Apostate caused the shrine of the holy martyr to be carried off, and the demon was able to speak. But, three months after, the temple of Apollo was consumed by lightning.

It is not unworthy of remark that sacred words and blessed things, which irritate and overcome the Devil, produce similar effects on objects which serve for spiritualistic conjurations. A table was seen to break asunder at the moment when a blessed rosary was, for the third time, laid upon it; a basket was seen, as related by the learned Abbé Bautain, formerly Vicar-General of Paris, to twist itself like a serpent and fly from the presence of a Gospel. If the employment of these means has not always an immediate success, it is that, then, as in the case of a priest exorcising one possessed, the Devil submits to suffer rather than confess himself vanquished. Against that immortal and infuriate enemy, no weapon gives here below a decisive victory, and our last hour shall be that of a final combat.

———

XXVI.

WHAT IS THE ADVANTAGE OF THE STATE
OF GRACE, IN THE STRUGGLE WITH THE
DEMON?

Every Christian is, by his own free
choice, in one or the other of these states:
the state of grace—the state of mortal sin.

Man, in the state of grace, is beloved
by God; he is united to Jesus Christ, as
the branch is to the trunk that nourishes
it with its sap: in his soul, the Father,
the Son, and the Holy Ghost do dwell,
lending him a habitual and uninterrupted
aid. It is true the devils prowl around
him—some of their darts may perchance
have wounded him; but he remains living
with a Divine life, because God, the true
life of every spirit, is in him, and with
him. Adopted son of the King of kings,
that Christian is *free.*

But as soon as the unhappy being has,
by a mortal transgression, wilfully broken

the bond of charity which united him to God, a frightful change is wrought. God withdraws His habitual aid; the branch severed from the trunk becomes barren. The Demon takes the place which the Lord, in departing, left vacant; he reigns there by right of conquest, and if the Saviour's mercy did not interpose, he would reign there for ever. A prodigal child, a rebel, a fugitive, that man is a *slave*.

Slave! The word is harsh, but it is correct. Pure spirits are stronger than the sons of Adam. Either the filial obedience to God which leads to glory and felicity; or subjection to Satan which works degradation and ruin! One day, Our Lord said to the Jews: "If you continue in my word, the truth shall make you free." The Jews, dissatisfied, answered: "We have never been slaves." Jesus answers them: "Amen, amen, I say unto you, that whosoever committeth sin, is the servant of sin. You say you are the children of God, but you have the Devil for your father, and the desires of your father you will do." (John, VIII, 31–44.)

The difference between the *soldier* fighting under the orders of an ever-victorious chief and a *slave* enchained by his most cruel enemy, is but the imperfect image of that which exists between the Christian in a state of grace and the Christian in mortal sin. The former, with a little vigilance, easily prevails over temptations; the latter, in order to resist his tyrant, requires heroic efforts and a very special aid from Jesus Christ. The *final* damnation of the reprobate was occasioned by this: *having too long neglected recovering the state of grace*, they were urged by the devils from one crime to another, even to the obduracy in which death struck them. To let those spirits of darkness abide in our soul, is to cast ourselves madly into the most evident danger of an eternal slavery: let us never forget this.

XXVII.

ON THE BREAD OF THE STRONG.

By baptism, God, Our Father, " delivers us from the power of darkness, and translates us into the kingdom of His beloved Son." (Col., I, 13.) By absolution, the bonds of malediction, which we had voluntarily tied again, are broken. For the Almighty Liberator has said to His lieutenants : " Whatsoever ye loose on earth, shall be loosed also in heaven." (St. Matth., XVIII, 18.) That is to say, the liberating sentences you shall pronounce here below shall be sanctioned above. To escape from the Devil, to avoid hell, the infidel must have recourse to *baptism;* the Christian to *confession.* But after

baptism, or absolution, all is not ended.
The Demon is going to return to the
charge.   Driven from the dwelling of
which sin had made him master, he says:
"'I will return into my house, whence I
have gone forth.'   And he goes back,
taking with him seven other spirits, more
wicked than himself," to reconquer it.
If he succeeds, the new state of that
man, overcome anew, shall be still more
wretched than the former.   Christian, you
have put him to flight; be watchful, then.
Most assuredly, the war will begin again.
Nevertheless, have confidence!   An all-
powerful ally knocks at the door of the
place and offers to defend it; that ally is
Jesus Christ in person, in the Eucharistic
mystery.

*The Holy Communion is the principal
and indispensable weapon of the Christian
in his spiritual combats with the infernal
powers;* it is because they either do not
receive Holy Communion, or receive it
badly, or too seldom, that the devils are

terrible to the frail children of Adam.* As soon as a Christian nourishes himself with the bread of the strong, as St. Vincent de Paul remarks, all is changed; that Christian returns from the Holy Table *"like a lion,* inflamed with Divine ardor, terrible to the demons,"* (these are the words of St. John Chrysostom;) and what wonder? That Christian marches to battle clothed not only with the armor furnished by Jesus Christ, but with Jesus Christ Himself! Hell may, doubtless, in its fury, assail him with desperate rage at the very moment when he receives his God; that has been seen, and is seen every day. But hell shall not enslave him. "HE WHO COMMUNICATES WELL, DOES ALL WELL," further said St. Vincent de Paul. Yes, he who communicates well, that is to say, frequently and worthily,

---

* Immediately after the sacrilegious communion of Judas, *Satan entered into him.* He who communicates badly, makes of the celestial bread *a deadly poison;* he who does not communicate, dies of *inanition.*

shall count his steps by victories; he shall keep the treasure of the holy and glorious liberty of the children of God, and his last struggle with hell shall be a splendid triumph.

O men, you who often complain of being tempted beyond your strength; you say that the assaults of the Devil are of irresistible violence. I well believe it. What would you say of the soldier who, in the midst of long and toilsome marches, combats by day and by night, would content himself with a piece of bread every two or three days, and complain of sinking under fatigue? "Take more nourishment," you would say to him. And I say to you: "Soldier of virtue, communicate oftener." A general law obliges every Christian to receive Holy Communion at Easter; the law of your conscience obliges you to communicate as often as you require in order to overcome the Devil. O men, understand, then, that in presence of your invisible enemies, as in that of your personal miseries, the *weaker* you feel yourselves, the greater is your need of having recourse often to the BREAD OF THE STRONG, to that Host which, in the combats of the spiritual life, is our strength, our help, our safety.*

XXVIII.

MARY, HELP OF CHRISTIANS.

All those who love the Mother of God, that is to say, all true Catholics, are persuaded that, after God, Mary is our principal support in our conflicts with Satan. This persuasion is not merely a pious conjecture; it rests on constant experience and on dogmatical foundations the most unshaken. After the fall of our first parents, the Devil who had seduced them heard the Lord say to him: " I will

* See, on this subject, so practical and of such grave importance, "*La Communion*," (The Communion,) by Mgr. de Ségur.

place enmity between the woman and thee, between her seed and thine; and THE WOMAN SHALL CRUSH THY HEAD, *ipsa conteret caput tuum*." (Gen., III, 15.) All the promises of God are fulfilled. Mary realized that a first time, by giving birth to the Man-God. But it is known that Mary was not, in that solemn hour, a blind instrument. She did, in the order of redemption, what Lucifer ought to have accomplished in the order of creation; she was, amongst creatures, *the first minister of God;* she was MOTHER, not only corporally, but also, and especially, in heart. Wherefore, more generously than any other, she took a willing and active part in the great work of the deliverance of mankind, enslaved by the Devil. Now, by a just requital, she contributes more effectually than any other, to the personal application of liberating grace to each of the souls of whom hell seeks to regain possession. Charity, the eternal law of the children of God, reigns

in paradise. Our triumphant brethren
do not forget us, and their affectionate
solicitude comes to our aid in the struggle we yet sustain; but, more powerful
and more loving than our brethren, that
glorious Mother covers us with a more
efficacious protection. After the name of
Jesus, no name is more terrible to hell
than hers. Mary has so often vanquished
our enemy and saved souls which, without her miraculous intervention, were lost,
that the Demon always trembles when
she is invoked.

"In a good family of Lille," says a
pious servant of Mary, "a young girl
named Catherine Dubus, became possessed of several devils, no one could tell
how or why. Only the external facts
could be known. When the terrible
guests who had seized upon her agitated
and dragged her about, six stout men
could not hold that young girl. Her
invisible enemies brought her to places
where she might cast herself down head-

long or drown herself; they dashed her against the walls as though trying hard to make away with her. They had depraved her senses to such a degree that she eat things that might kill her, sought for poisons, and chewed stones. Had she been a poor girl, people would not have been wanting who suspected some fearful jugglery for the purpose of making money; but strong-minded people had not even this resource, for Catherine belonged to a family in easy circumstances.

"She was taken to the shrine of Our Lady of Montaigu, (in Belgium); she is exorcised before the image of Mary. During the imposing ceremony, the demoniac was seen to throw off her bewitched stomach needles, stones, nails, brimstone. She was heard to utter strange words and reveal unknown facts. Several times she exhaled puffs of smoke, which went forth from her mouth and vanished. She was delivered."

Who is the first author that relates

this? Justus Lipsus, who, with Scaliger and Casaubon, formed that famous triumvirate of learned men in the second half of the sixteenth century.

Whilst yet young, and already attacked furiously by the Devil, who foresaw in him a terrible adversary, Francis de Sales was tormented by a thought of despair. One day, he at length regains peace . . . before an image of Mary, whom he had invoked.*

But what is the use of multiplying examples? Here is a fact which is under the eyes of all. To-day, amongst us, thousands of young girls, even amid the perils of poverty, of ignorance, of destitution, resist all the assaults of hell, and not only keep their reputation untouched, but their heart pure. Whence comes this prodigy? It is that they are *children of Mary!* And their triumph is entirely the work of the tutelary Virgin

* This statue is venerated in the chapel of the Ladies of St. Thomas of Villanova, in Paris.

that no sooner do they wilfully give up their pious assemblies, than these poor children forget God, duty, virtue, and fall like others!

The powers of the abyss know better than we how formidable to them is the Mother of their Conqueror. They have experienced the virtue of the "Hail Mary," of the "*Memorare*," of the beads, of the scapular, of that little medal which recalls the memory of the spotless Virgin. We all remember the outburst of blasphemy that greeted, seventeen years ago, the Definition of the Immaculate Conception. What harm was done to the wicked and the unbelieving by the decree of the Church declaring Mary exempt from that original stain which, according to them, does not exist? But hell trembled, seeing Mary honored; and by the mouth, and pen, and arm of those who follow its inspirations, it exhaled its fury. Well! its conduct is a lesson for us; it detests the Virgin most pure : we will love her! It would have her forgotten: we will every where proclaim her greatness! It fears her: we will invoke her with filial confidence! She shall crush the head of the old serpent: she will be for us *Our Lady of Victory!*

XXIX.

OF ANGELICAL ASSISTANCE.

"The angels," says St. Paul, "are ministering spirits, sent to minister for those who shall receive the inheritance of salvation." (Heb., I, 14.) This is not the place to enumerate all the occasions wherein Holy Writ and history show the tutelary power of the faithful angels in operation. In the ninetieth Psalm, (*cum invocarum,*) we see the just man defended against the arrows that fly in the darkness and against the noon-day devil. No evil shall come to him; nor shall the scourge come near his dwelling. But how? God has commanded His angels to keep him in all his ways; in their hands they bear him up, lest he dash his foot against a stone. From the celebrated saying of Our Lord Jesus Christ, declaring that even little children have, to protect them, angels who see the face of the Heavenly Father, holy doctors and theologians have deduced, by plain reasoning, the belief in the *Guardian Angel*. It is probable enough that each of us is more particularly attacked by one devil, as we are each specially guarded by one faithful spirit. Against the angel of darkness, recourse must be had to the angel of light. He lacks neither zeal nor power; but a general law of Providence so arranges that all assistance from above comes from God directly, either by angels and saints, associated in the government and sanctification of mankind, or demanded by humble, respectful, trusting prayer.

How charming is that story of the Angel Raphael, which even little children know! In two cities far distant from each other, two pious families were in affliction. Tobias was blind, poor, persecuted. Raguel had seen the young men to whom he had successively given the hand of Sara, his daughter, die a violent death, slain, the Scripture says, by the devil Asmodeus. God sends His angel, St. Raphael, to bring back joy to these two sorrowing households. The young Tobias has to go to Rages; Raphael, under the appearance of a youthful stranger, offers to be his guide. One day, as Tobias is washing his feet in the Tigris, an enormous fish darts upon him. "Take him," says the mysterious guide, "and draw him to thee." Tobias obeys, and keeps the heart and liver of the fish, according to the orders he received. *Chance,* as frivolous people would say, PROVIDENCE, says reason enlightened by faith, brings Tobias to the house of Raguel. Tobias marries Sara: they spend the three first nights after the wedding

in prayer; the devil is expelled by the
angel. Tobias returns to his aged father
with Raguel's wealth, and cures his blindness by the application of the fish's gall.
The two families are happy. The heavenly messenger at length makes himself
known; he gives affectionate advice to
those whom he has protected, and dis-
appears.

Many Saints, since the time of Jesus
Christ, have enjoyed favors similar to
those which Tobias received. Rome, the
city of admirable memories, still shows,
on the Plaza Navona, the spot where St.
Agnes, a child of twelve years, dragged
by the executioners to a house of infamy,
found *the angel whom the Lord had prepared* to defend her.

The angel of the Indies appeared to
St. Francis Xavier, to exhort him to
carry the Gospel courageously to those
countries where, after fifteen centuries of
Christianity, the devils were still univers-
ally worshipped.

In fine, wherever God exercises His bounty, the ministers of that bounty interfere the more actively, according as our recourse to their fraternal support is more ardent and tender. Their delight, like that of the incarnate Word, their Chief, is doing good.

Let us, then, know how to repeat, with the Church, that invocation with which the public office every evening concludes: "Visit, O Lord, this habitation; drive far from it all snares of the enemy; let Thy holy angels dwell therein, and Thy blessing be upon us for ever. Through Christ Our Lord."

At a period when the audacity and influence of the demons are redoubled, devotion to the holy angels ought to revive. Now more than ever should the priest, the Christian mother, inculcate it to the young souls whom God confides to them, in order that a thorough Christian education may raise them up to Him.

XXX.

FINAL DESTINY OF THE VICTORS AND THE VANQUISHED.

The present life is a conflict that lasts from dawn till night. Whatever may be the number of his victories, the just man may still fall, if he cease to struggle; whatever may be the number of his defeats, the sinner may rise again, if, from the depth of his misery, he cries to God, his support. But death comes at last. And then? . . . Then? say those spirits who, for some years, come so willingly to chat with the curious who listen to them—then? People shall begin a new life in a new sphere, where they shall be lodged according to their previous merits: and from that new hostelry, they shall pass on, by a new death, indefinitely to another. That if one sometimes turn away from God by disobedience, he need not be very much troubled, because Our Creator, let us do what we may, must and will give us felicity. Those spirits know well what they are about. To say that evil shall remain unpunished, would be too much; it would horrify men! To say that the punishment shall be light and easy, is all that is necessary to make mankind, never much afraid of any purgatory whatsoever — putting off to some one of those numerous existences promised to it, the fulfilment of God's commandments — always answer those who preach virtue: "To-morrow, to-morrow."

Christianity, that teaching brought from heaven by a God, and attested by so many prophecies and miracles; Christianity, which, by the splendor of the proof of all kinds which it brought in support of its truth, made itself acceptable, in spite of the sacrifices it requires, by the Pagan and by the barbarian world; Christianity, which has withstood eighteen centuries of attack; Christianity, in which we must believe, if we believe in anything—Christianity maintains, against this renewal of the errors of India, of Pythagoras, the decree of the Apostle: "It is appointed for men once to die, and after this the judgment." (Heb., IX, 27.)

God does not permit men to mock Him and imitate the scholar who says: "My master will punish me, I know; but, no matter, I am going to carry out my own notion; punishment will come after, and when it is over, I shall have got the better of the master; I shall have done my own will, and, in spite of his punishment, I shall have been the strongest." The faculty of disobeying God, that is to say, of doing under the eyes of God, and with the power we hold from God, that which God forbids, is granted to intelligent beings for a time, *in order that trial may be made*, and merit acquired; but this astonishing position is not to last always; war between the Creator and the creature is not the normal state of creation. After having regarded the contest for some time, God says: "It is enough."

And death goes in search of the combatants, whom it brings before His judgment-seat. There, each one is judged, and introduced into the house of his eternity.

What does the victorious Christian find in that house of eternity? A glory and a bliss which he shall enjoy in assured peace.

"He that hath an ear, let him hear what the spirit saith: To him that overcometh, I will give to eat of the tree of life which is in the paradise of my God. Behold, the Devil shall cast some of you into prison, that you may be tried. Be thou faithful unto death, and I will give thee the crown of life. To him that overcometh, I will give the hidden manna, a new name which no man knoweth, but he that receiveth it. . . . He that shall overcome, shall be clothed in white garments, and I will confess his name before my Father, and before His angels. . . . He that shall overcome, I will make him a pillar in the temple of my God, and he shall go out no more. . . . To him that shall overcome, I will grant to sit with me in my throne." (Apoc., II and III.)

God, whose infinite power is equaled by His infinite generosity, will not be sparing in the reward of the man who shall have fought the good fight; Himself will be the eternal joy of His faithful servant.

But what shall happen to him whom death shall surprise loaded with the chains of Satan, become, through malice or through cowardice, the companion and slave of the revolted spirits? In vain will he allege the strength of his enemies. He had been enrolled under the banner of an ever-victorious Chief. An Apostle had told him: "Be subject to God, but resist the Devil, and he will fly from you." (St. James, IV, 7.) Another Apostle had warned him that the sting of Satan must be opposed by the grace of Jesus Christ. (II Cor., XII, 7, 9.) It was sufficient for him to look around him and

consider the just in their ways to know
that a Liberator exists. He preferred
the shame of a slothful bondage to the
hardships of the fight. That which he
chose of his own free will is now imposed
upon him; he shall remain far from the
God he has forsaken, far from the cour-
ageous soldiers of the Lord from whom
he separated; he shall be banished to
the lowest depths of creation with the
masters he has preferred, because they
favored his passions, to the God who, for
him, died on a cross. There is the future
of the wilfully conquered.

And, in the lapse of ages, an hour will
come—the last—when all creation shall
be summoned to hear the judgment of
every creature pronounced. Then the
Man-God shall appear surrounded by
His faithful angels, and He shall say to
the victorious: "Come, ye blessed of my
Father, possess the kingdom prepared
for you from the beginning of the world."
And to the conquered: "Go, ye cursed,

into everlasting fire, prepared for the Devil and his angels." Immediately, the last separation shall take place : the victors shall go into "life everlasting," the conquered into "everlasting punishment." (St. Matth., xxv.)

Thenceforward, no more combatants ; but the just rewarded and the wicked punished. The triumph of good over evil will be final, complete, eternal.

XXXI.

ADVICE TO THOSE WHO BELIEVE, AND TO THOSE WHO BELIEVE NOT.

Now, dear readers, we must conclude. The misfortune of most men is that they know not how to conclude. They hear a discourse, they read a book, and go to their business, or their pleasures without having asked themselves : "What is the result of this in relation to my personal conduct? What is the warning that Providence now gives me?"

The question of the Devil is not one of mere curiosity. The question is of a living enemy, powerful, present, dangerous, furious. You are reminded that he has caused the terrible, irremediable ruin of a multitude of your fellow-beings. You are warned, in particular, to avoid dark associations, inspired by him, mysterious operations, of which he himself (as often as jugglery is not the sole mover) is the invisible agent.

When flight is impossible, fight. Avoid more carefully even those trivial faults which make the Devil bolder and stronger against you; avoid, especially, mortal sin, which would deliver your soul to him. Never sleep, if you possibly can, in the captivity of Satan. Be on your guard against the love of riches, which fills his nets; the love of pleasure, which leads to idolatry; and pride, the father of all errors. Grieve not the Spirit of God. Watch, pray. Soon you shall repose in the triumphant peace of heaven.

If you have the misfortune not to share our belief, be prudent, and do not rush into intimacy with mysterious beings whose sincerity and good faith you cannot possibly verify. Wait till those spirits have ceased to give the unedifying sight of a confused mixture of the true and the false, the grave and the ridiculous, of devout conversations and immoral conversations. At least, begin by reading attentively the books published by distinguished men who have studied this question coolly and according to the rules of sound criticism—the learned works of Messrs. de Mirville, Desmousseaux, Bizouard, from which we have been able to borrow but little. Meditate, at least, on the solid pamphlets of M. de Roys, Père Matignon, Abbé Tilloy, and Père Pailloux. Ignorance is not excusable, when instruction is to be had; and heedlessness is very unreasonable, when there is question of our immortal soul.

APPENDIX.

APPENDIX.

A.

I.

M. de Tristan, a distinguished member of several learned societies, had seen, at first, in table-turning, only an electric fact; but in April, 1853, he wrote to M. de Mirville: "Dating from the day when a light table unexpectedly took to rapping, this wonder specially attracted our attention. . . . It became *impossible for me to doubt* that this phenomenon was due to some agency.

"The greater part of the time, it is true, we had but little fault to find with these *metaphysical intervening beings*, because we act with extreme caution; but, little by little, the numerous falsehoods, at first of no importance, became more grave, calumnies were multiplied, proposals of intimacy, of *engagement*, of good-fellowship, joined with some doubtful opinions, began to excite our suspicions. For my part, I am not only convinced of this intervention, but *I have obtained the avowal that all these beings are banished for ever from the presence of God.*"

II.

"I have seen tables turn. . . . I have heard them speak in their own way. There are there phenomena of intelligence, of will, of liberty, . . . and such causes have always been called *spirits*. But what spirits? It is certain, in the first place, that these spirits see and know things of which we are ignorant and which we cannot see. These facts are reproduced from day to day. . . . The spirits in question, then, see more and farther than we do, and if they do not always see right and speak truly, it remains certain that, without being infallible, they see things belonging to the other world which we perceive not. . . . From what I have seen and heard, I say confidently that they are not good spirits. I want but one proof, and for me it is decisive; it is, that they refuse to answer clearly in what concerns Our Lord Jesus Christ, and when they are urged to do so by an imperative order, the tables resist, shake, raise themselves up, and sometimes turn over and throw themselves on the ground, escaping from the hands that touch them. . . . I have seen these things many times; I one day saw a basket thus agitated, twisting like a serpent, and fly creeping away before a book of the Gospels held out to it without anything being said." (M. Bautain, Vicar-General of Paris, Doctor of Theology, Law, and Medicine.)

III.

"At the house of one of my friends, an eminent physician," says M. de Mirville, "the pencil wrote, word for word,

this sentence : ' If you will give yourself
up to me, soul and body, I will crown all
your desires, even that which you have
most at heart, at this moment. If you
consent, sign your name under mine, and
that will suffice.' . . . And the spirit
signed *Gielf*."

IV.

M. de Sauley, of the Institute, who,
after a long term of unbelief, at length
yielded to evidence, also saw himself con-
tinually solicited to *engage*. He believed
himself in connection with two spirits.
One, violent, blustering, blaspheming, insolent, advised, and did nothing but what
was bad; the other, very smooth and
gentle, disputed with the first, and made
edification succeed to scandal. But behold when, summoned to explain how it
was, this excellent spirit, after a struggle
of two hours, replies: "Poor dupe, you
thought you had two of us, and you had
but one ; I was alone."

V.

Facts which occurred at Rauzan (Gironde) in 1853. *Extract from the answers obtained by Viscount de Meslon, and facts relating thereto:*

" *Q.* Is it really with intelligent beings we have to do?—*A.* Yes. *Q.* Are you good spirits?—*A.* Yes. *Q.* Is there an everlasting hell?—*A.* No. *Q.* Does the Catholic religion, then, deceive us on that point?—*A.* Yes. *Q.* In what does the punishment of the wicked consist?—*A.* In going to pass a shorter or longer time of trial in the sphere nearest the earth, then to rise successively and progressively from sphere to sphere, according as the spirit is purified, till at length it reaches the last sphere, and is reunited to God. *Q.* Are you of the same nature as the spirit-rappers of the United States?—*A.* Yes."

Soon after a spirit declares himself the brother of M. de Meslon, who died in

1845, in great sentiments of religion, and answers with the utmost precision all the questions put to him in consequence of this announcement. He is adjured, *in the name of the living God*, not to deceive, and crucifixes and blessed objects are placed on the table. The spirit persists in saying that he was sent by God to enlighten his family, to defend it against the snares of the devils, and to guide it in the way of virtue and of truth. Every moment, he quotes, of himself, sentences from Holy Writ, urges his hearers to love God and to honor the Blessed Virgin. When he is asked questions relating to financial matters, or the future, he strenuously refuses to answer, and admonishes, in the name of God, those who interrogate him, as to their lightness and imprudence.

But, one evening, a small work-table, questioned in its turn, advises distrust of the spirit of the round table. The latter replies by summoning, *in the name of the living God*, the spirit of the work-table to confess that he is the spirit of evil. After an obstinate resistance and some fearful contortions, the little table avows that it is animated by the Devil, envious of the good which the departed soul was doing to his family. "Thenceforward," says M. de Meslon, "our confidence would have been absolute, when God, who saw the depth of our hearts, no longer permitted the devil to deceive us. One Sunday, the little round table, which almost always spoke of itself, at first refused to answer, then rose up impatiently, and said to us these words *verbatim:* 'I am tired repeating to you incessantly honeyed words which I do not think, and expressing affectionate sentiments, when I have no feeling for you but hatred.' 'But are you not him whom you pretend to be?' we asked in amazement. 'No.' 'Who are you, then?' '*The spirit of evil.*' 'What was the object of the disgraceful farce you have been so long playing with us?' ' *Seeking to inspire you with confidence, the better to deceive you afterwards.*' 'But did you not suffer at being obliged to speak to us of God, the Virgin, and the Saints, and especially when a crucifix, religious medals, etc , were laid on the table?' ' I suffered, but concealed my suffering in the hope of succeeding afterwards in leading you astray.' ' You hate us, then?' ' Yes, because you are Christians.' Then the spirit took leave of us with these words: ' God *forces* me to speak thus; hell claims me back; farewell.'"

These facts are related more at length, with others quite as significant, in M. de Mirville's *Question des Esprits*, (Spirit Question,) a work which cannot be too highly commended to well-disposed people who, being deceived, do not recognize the wolf in sheep's clothing. Every being that holds wicked discourse is necessarily wicked; but he who says good things is not necessarily good: clever hypocrisy borrows the language of virtue, and even of piety, so as easily to be mistaken for them. The name of God, carelessly put forward through rash curiosity, does not frighten the evil spirits; employed without much faith, it does not immediately triumph over their pride. Finally, every being, whether man or spirit, who advances a doctrine, on questions of vital importance to mankind, concerning its duties or its future, ought to furnish rational demonstration, or prove clearly that he is sent by God. Our invisible gossips have neither one nor the other. Their philosophy is not more solid than that of any dreamer of flesh and bone. And very far from furnishing proof of a Divine mission, they are often compelled, as in the first days of Christianity, to show *the tips of their horns*. Spiritists who are in good faith, use habitually, and with perfectly pure intention, the Sign of the Cross; the mask will fall from your *good spirits!* If you reject a practice so easy, you have only yourselves to blame for your blindness.

B.

THE TRANSMIGRATION OF SOULS.

"Give us," said a person to spirit-rappers, "some idea of Divine goodness." "How could I, since it is infinite?" "It is infinite, and yet you suffer, unhappy one!" "Cruelly." "And for ever?" "For ever." "But, wretched as you appear to be, and God being as good as you say, suppose you tried to soften Him —who knows?" "You ask what would be absolutely impossible." "And why?" "He cannot pardon me, *since I do not want him to do so.*" "And if He proposed complete annihilation, would you accept it?" After some hesitation one of the spirits replies: "*Yes, because being is the only good I still hold from Him, and then, being no longer anything, I should be free of Him.*" The other said: "*No, I*

*would not accept, because I should no longer
have the consolation of hating Him.*" "Do
you, then, hate so?" "*Do I hate?* . . .
Why, my name is hatred; I hate all; I
hate myself."* . . .

To this instance of candor on the part
of reprobate spirits, we might add several avowals forced from them by exorcisms or the power of a lively faith; but
usually, as St. Augustine observed in the
fifth century, those proud deceivers deny
their reprobation, and especially its eternal duration. In our days, spirit-rappers work with as much energy as unani-
mity to replace the doctrine of an eternal
hell by that of the migration of souls,
called by the Greeks metempsychosis.
According to Herodotus, this doctrine
originated amongst the Egyptians, who
taught it to the Greek philosopher Pythagoras, whence it passed into the writ-
ings of Plato. The Druid priests of the
Celts appear also to have been infatuated

* *Question des Esprits*, ch. III.

with this error, which, after having vanished before the light of Christianity,
reappeared only amongst some Eastern
heretics, who would fain have made a
confused mixture of Plato and the Gospel. After a long enough sleep, it has
again raised its head; in Germany, in
the works of the pantheist Krause, and
in France, in those of Fourier.

According to Fourier, "after the present life, each soul, whatever may have
been its conduct, takes possession of a
delightful existence in a subtile body
named aroma. Supporting itself in the
air, and going through, without an effort,
the hardest bodies, the aromal body con-
tinually feels sensations as delicious as
varied." The author declares that if all
men *would hasten to kill themselves*, they
would understand the superiority of this
other existence. "Each and every soul
shall pass twenty-seven thousand years
on the earth, and fifty-four thousand in
other celestial bodies, after which it shall

be absorbed in the soul of the earth."
The author of *Terre et Ciel*, (Earth and
Heaven,) Jean Reynaud, has reproduced,
spiritualizing it, this dream of the metempsychosis, and, lastly, the spirit-rappers
proclaim it as the final key of human
destiny. But this migration of souls is
not only unproved, but not even likely.
In fact, as M. H. Martin de Rennes judiciously observes,* "to propose to the
human soul endless trials, instead of
one decisive trial, is to diminish the
hope that encourages, and the fear that
prevents us from doing evil and perse-
vering therein."

Besides, if God had given us this
strange destiny, He would apparently
have apprised us of it. But no, the
migration of souls has, in its favor, a
small number of dreamers, reinforced by
invisible goblins, who, with their other
little accomplishments, tell people's age,

* *La vie future, suivant la foi et la religion.* (The Future Life, according to Faith and Religion.)

make tables dance the polka, sketch
devils in miniature, play the piano, beat
the drum, etc., together with that of revealing the past and the future, without
government security. For the Christian,
there is no question of it. For even the
unbeliever, if he reflects, the persistence
with which the spirit-rappers preach the
transmigration of souls ought to make
that fantastic dream still more suspicious.
What! to run from planet to planet, or
else to be on this globe successively man,
mouse, turkey, crocodile, poodle, mule,
elephant, would be the destiny of mankind; and mankind, deaf to the specious
arguments of half a dozen philosophers,
would have waited till, in the middle of
the nineteenth century, tables beat the
générale, to know it! . . . If there is a
hell, a hard and an ignominious prison
for insolent criminals, spirits jealous of
man, will they enter into communication
with us to proclaim their shame, and
revive in our souls the saving fear of the

punishment they are undergoing? In a jail, are not the prisoners all honest people, victims of mistaken justice? Let Messrs. Pelletan, Jourdan, Laurent, and other worshippers of this nineteenth century, convinced that before Voltaire and Rousseau, the thickest darkness covered the earth, gravely discuss and maintain such Utopian fancies, if they will; let the Book of the Spirits (*Livre des Esprits*) come to their aid as Satan came to the aid of Luther in famous nightly conversations; the metempsychosis shall always remain what it has been at all times: a chimera of the imagination, rejected, at the same time, by Christian revelation, the traditions of mankind, and good sense. Christianity teaches that the human soul, made to be united with a body, shall find again, after a temporary separation, its body, to which it shall be thenceforth reunited, for ever, in heaven or in hell. There is the truth.

C.

THE DEVIL'S ADVOCATES IN THE NINE-
TEENTH CENTURY.

Every period has its miseries. The misery of our time is the so-called philosophical justification of evil. Our ancestors, too, knew human frailty, but they did not canonize disorder; and when they yielded to the unhappy inclinations of the flesh, they did not place it, with the august name of REASON, on an altar. We have progressed, and the justification of evil brings, now-a-days, its natural consequence—the restoration of Satan, who first committed evil, and inspires it in us.

Milton, an English poet of lofty genius, but thoroughly imbued with the spirit of the so-called Reformation, in his great poem "Paradise Lost," painted the demons, and especially their chief, as of grand and beautiful physiognomy, although not attempting to excuse them.

Literature and the Stage caught up Milton's idea, and, carrying it still farther, re-opened the gates of heaven to the Devil, disguised as an interesting victim. "Long live hell!" (*Vive l'enfer!*) cried the slayers of priests and the demolishers of churches in 1793. And that savage cry has more than once been heard at the period of more recent social commotions; it has been raised, in Switzerland, as a war-cry against the Catholics. But all is eclipsed by the versification of the thinker who has written the "Contemplations." The philosophy of M. Hugo reduces itself to metempsychosis extending to all. All suffers, but all is going helter-skelter to joy. We must love all, esteem all, even the worst scoundrels; there can be no exception—but the race of *devotees.*

According to him, the instrument of crime, and the bolt that secures the criminal in his prison, alike share his sufferings and the sufferings of his victim.

Pity the prisoner, but pity the bolt.

* * * * * *

The axe suffers as much as the body ; the blood
Suffers as much as the head, O mysteries from on high !

Thanks to these sufferings, (very mysterious, truly !) every criminal makes his own punishment.

And the thorn, Caiaphas, and the reed, Pilate. . .
Cry out to the Adorable Being. . .
The vulture says to the sparrow in the shade : Pardon !
Of their crimes the stones are heard to accuse themselves,
And, under the softened eye looking down from above,
The whole abyss is but one immense sob. . .

Before this immense sob of vultures and stones, of the wicked become shrubs, and axes saddened by the bloody trade they are made to ply, divine justice must feel itself disarmed. "Universal softening is the prologue of universal reconciliation. Hydras shall be seen emerging from the abyss, with stars on their foreheads ; horns shall be changed into aureolas ; claws shall hold palms ; the damned shall go up to heaven, Belial at their head; finally, Jesus shall embrace Belial his brother, and lead him to God."—(*Louis Veuillot.*)

Both shall be so beautiful that God's own flaming eye
Can no longer distinguish, delighted Father as he is,
Belial from Jesus!

Very good for M. Victor Hugo! The Supreme Intelligence so dazzled that it will no longer distinguish the Holy of holies from the worker of all evil! And yet there are people who read this blasphemous nonsense, and do not say: "It is absurd!" The restoration of the invisible disgraced one is become, in the unbelieving world, a sort of accomplished fact, *big with threats for the future.*

But a word on the two best known advocates of poor Satan. The first is M. Proudhon; the second, M. Renan.

M. Proudhon sums himself up in his frightful formula: *God is evil.* According to this reckoning, Satan must be good.

A finished type of the perfect revolutionary, M. Proudhon has a system well connected in all its parts. This system consists in taking all things the very contrary of the true and the good, as announced by reason and conscience; thence his tenderness for Satan, whom he admires, and would be happy to resemble. In his book on "The Church and the Revolution," he has written these lines, which no baptized hand of man, says Padre Ventura, referring to them, had written before:

"Come, Satan, come, calumniated of priests and kings, that I may embrace thee, that I may clasp thee to my breast! *Long have I known thee, and thou me, too.* Thy works, O blessed of my heart, are not always either fair or good, but they alone give a meaning to the universe, and prevent it from being absurd. . . . Thou ennoblest riches . . . thou puttest the seal on virtue . . . I have but one pen to serve thee, but it is worth millions of bulletins, and I here vow to lay it down only when the days sung by the poet (*the days of Paganism apparently, the days when Satan was worshipped*) shall have come again."

M. Renan, of a very different character, neither knows how to hate God nor love Satan with such frightful energy. But in his "Studies on Religious History," (where he invents history and religion,) he offers, like a *bouquet*, (*àpropos* to a picture of Scheffer's,) a sentimental plea in favor of said "calumniated," who is made out the most interesting personage imaginable, *an unsuccessful revolutionary*, a Poërio of the first ages! This reversal of opinion is presented as the fair fruit of toleration and of modern lights.

"Of all beings, formerly accused, whom the toleration of our age has freed from his anathema, Satan is, undeniably, the one who has gained most by the progress of light and of universal civilization." (M. Renan does not here pretend to let fly a sharp arrow against certain lights and certain civilization.) "The Middle Ages, which heard nothing of toleration, made him, at pleasure, wicked, tormented, and, worst disgrace of all, ridiculous." The *high impartiality* of our age has changed all that. Reader, you would never guess the reason, especially if you remember that M. Renan, like the inferior beings of creation, *ignores the existence of God*, and has so little tact as to boast of it: it is *through respect for God!* "We who respect the divine spark wherever it is found, hesitate to pronounce exclusive warrants, for fear of involving in our condemnation some atom of beauty." And, in fact, M. Renan finds, in Satan, not only an "atom of beauty," but a great and ravishing beauty. Satan is the *bad*, the organizer of evil, and evil, for M. Renan, is much more artistic, with its vivid and striking shades, than good. which, according to him, is uniform and monotonous. More fortunate than Proudhon, M. Renan has received his fees : he is *High Chancellor of the great Orient of France !*

So much absurdity confounds, so much audacity excites a legitimate indignation. Yet logic there leads to an impious fellowship ; the enemies of those we love not seem to us friends. The revolt against God, the wretch who hates God in proportion to the fear wherewith the justice of God inspires him, sees in Satan a rebel like himself—like him, an enemy of God. He feels a sympathy for Satan. Let the devils again demand altars, they will obtain them ; the Pantheist choir, with M. Victor Hugo for leader, will sing hymns in honor of the ancient rebels ; the phalanx of the independent, guided by M. Proudhon, will relieve those who refused submission even to their Creator ; and the tribe of Atheists, by the light of the phosphorescent phrases of M. Renan, will wonder at the rich variety of these innumerable quasi-gods. Paganism, demanded again by blinded men, shall be restored to them, and society shall fall back into barbarism, miraculously overcome by Christianity. My God, forgive these wretches; they know not him whose cause they plead, they know not what they do! . . .

EXORCISM

Against Satan and the Rebellious Angels

*Published by order of
His Holiness, Pope Leo XIII.*

The Holy Father exhorts priests to say this prayer as often as possible, as a simple exorcism to curb the power of the devil and prevent him from doing harm. The faithful also may say it in their own name for the same purpose, as any approved prayer. Its use is recommended whenever action of the devil is suspected, causing malice in men, violent temptations, and even storms and various calamities. It could be used as a solemn exorcism (an official and public ceremony, in Latin) to expel the devil. It would then be said by a priest, in the name of the Church, and only with the Bishop's permission.

IN THE NAME of the Father and of the Son and of the Holy Ghost. Amen.

Prayer to St. Michael the Archangel

Glorious Prince of the Celestial Host, St. Michael the Archangel, defend us in the conflict which we have to sustain "against principalities and powers, against the rulers of the world of this darkness, against the spirits of wickedness in the high places." *(Ephes. 6:12)*. Come to the rescue of men, whom God has created to His image and likeness, and whom He has redeemed at a great price from the tyranny of the devil. It is thou whom Holy Church venerates as her guardian and her protector, thou whom the Lord has charged to conduct redeemed souls into Heaven. Pray, therefore, the God of Peace to subdue Satan beneath our feet, that he may no longer retain men captive nor do injury to the Church. Present our prayers to the Most High, that without delay they may draw His mercy down upon us. Seize "the dragon, the old serpent, which is the devil and Satan," bind him and cast him into the bottomless pit ". . . that he [may] no more seduce the nations." *(Apoc. 20:2-3)*.

Exorcism

In the Name of Jesus Christ, our Lord and Saviour, strengthened by the intercession of the Immaculate Virgin Mary, Mother of God, of Blessed Michael the Archangel, of the Blessed Apostles Peter and Paul, and all the Saints, and powerful in the holy authority of our ministry, we confidently undertake to repulse the attacks and deceits of the devil.

Let God arise, and let His enemies be scattered: and let them that hate Him flee from before His face.

As smoke vanisheth, so let them vanish away: as wax melteth before the fire, so let the wicked perish at the presence of God. *(Psalm 67:2-3)*.

V. Behold the Cross of the Lord! Flee, bands of enemies.

R. The Lion of the Tribe of Juda, the Offspring of David, hath conquered.

V. May Thy mercy descend upon us.

R. As great as our hope in Thee.

We drive you from us, whoever you may be, unclean spirits, Satanic powers, infernal invaders, wicked legions, assemblies and sects. In the name and by the virtue of Our Lord Jesus Christ ✠, may you be snatched away and driven from the Church of God and from the souls redeemed by the Precious Blood of the Divine Lamb ✠. Cease by your audacity, cunning serpent, to delude the human race, to persecute the Church, to torment God's elect, and to sift them as wheat ✠. This is the command made to you by the Most High God ✠, with Whom in your haughty insolence you still pretend to be equal ✠, the God "Who will have all men to be saved, and to come to the knowledge of the truth." *(1 Tim. 2:4).* God the Father commands you ✠; God the Son commands you ✠; God the Holy Ghost commands you ✠. Christ commands you, the Eternal Word of God made Flesh; He Who to save our race, out-done through your malice, "humbled Himself, becoming obedient unto death" *(Phil. 2:8);* He Who has built His Church on the firm rock and declared that the gates of Hell shall not prevail against her, because He dwells with her "all days, even to the consummation of the world." *(Matt. 28:20).* The hidden virtue of the Cross requires it of you as does also the power of the mysteries of the Christian Faith ✠. The glorious Mother of God, the Virgin Mary, commands you ✠; she who by her humility and from the first moment of her Immaculate Conception crushed your proud head. The faith of the holy Apostles Peter and Paul and of the other Apostles commands you ✠. The blood of the martyrs and the pious intercession of all the Saints command you ✠.

Thus, cursed dragon, and you, wicked legions, we adjure you by the living God ✠, by the true God ✠, by the holy God ✠, by the God Who "so loved the world, as to give His only-begotten Son; that whosoever believeth in Him, may not perish but may have life everlasting." *(Jn. 3:16)*. Cease deceiving human creatures and pouring out to them the poison of eternal perdition; cease harming the Church and hindering her liberty. Retreat, Satan, inventor and master of all deceit, enemy of man's salvation. Cede the place to Christ in Whom you have found none of your works. Cede the place to the One, Holy, Catholic, and Apostolic Church acquired by Christ at the price of His Blood. Stoop beneath the all-powerful Hand of God, tremble and flee at the invocation of the holy and terrible Name of Jesus, this Name which causes Hell to tremble, this name to which the Virtues, Powers, and Dominations of Heaven are humbly submissive, this name which the Cherubim and Seraphim praise unceasingly, repeating: Holy, Holy, Holy is the Lord, the God of hosts.

V. O Lord, hear my prayer.
R. And let my cry come unto Thee.

V. May the Lord be with thee.
R. And with thy spirit.

Let Us Pray

God of Heaven, God of earth, God of Angels, God of Archangels, God of Patriarchs, God of Prophets, God of Apostles, God of Martyrs, God of Confessors, God of Virgins, God Who hast power to give life after death and rest after work, because there is no other God than Thee and there can be no other, for Thou art the Creator of all things, visible and invisible, of Whose reign there shall be no end, we humbly prostrate ourselves before Thy glorious majesty and we supplicate Thee to deliver us from all the tyranny of the infernal spirits, from their snares, and their furious wickedness. Deign, O Lord, to protect us by Thy power and to preserve us safe and sound. We beseech Thee through Jesus Christ our Lord. Amen.

From the snares of the devil, deliver us, O Lord.

That Thy Church may serve Thee in peace and liberty, We beseech Thee to hear us.

That Thou wouldst crush down all enemies of Thy Church, We beseech Thee to hear us.

(Holy Water is sprinkled in the place where we may be.)

IMPRIMATUR: Manuel, Bishop of Barcelona
December 19, 1931

Prayer to St. Michael

Composed by Pope Leo XIII (1878-1903)
and formerly said after low Mass in Catholic churches.

Saint Michael, the Archangel, defend us in battle; be our defense against the wickedness and snares of the devil. May God rebuke him, we humbly pray; and do thou, O Prince of the heavenly host, by the power of God, thrust into Hell Satan and the other evil spirits who prowl about the world for the ruin of souls. Amen.

NIHIL OBSTAT: John A. Goodwine, J.C.D.
                 Censor Librorum

IMPRIMATUR: Francis Cardinal Spellman
                 Archbishop of New York
                 February 24, 1961

OTHER TITLES AVAILABLE